Nel

Much Ado
About Nothing

Nelson Thornes Shakespeare

Much Ado About Nothing

Volume editor: **Lawrence Green**

Series editors: **Duncan Beal and Dinah Jurksaitis**

Series consultant: **Peter Thomas**

Published in 2004 by:
Nelson Thornes Ltd
Delta Place
27 Bath Road
CHELTENHAM
GL53 7TH
United Kingdom

04 05 06 07 08 / 10 9 8 7 6 5 4 3 2 1

A catalogue record for this book is available from the British Library.

ISBN 0-7487-8603-1

Illustration by Peters and Zabransky

Page make-up by Tech-set

Printed and bound in Spain by GraphyChems

Acknowledgements

Bridgeman Art Library (www.bridgeman.co.uk)/The Stapleton Collection, p.8; Mary Evans Picture Library, p.12; Moviestore, p.34; Shakespeare Birthplace Trust, pp. 58, 74, 90, 104, 106, 114.

Contents

Preface   **vi**

Foreword   **vii**

Introductory essays   **1**

1 Women in a man's world   **1**

2 Wooing and wiving   **4**

3 Formalities and festivities   **7**

4 Valour, honour and the *duello*   **10**

5 Crime and punishment   **13**

The characters   **17**

Play text   **18**

Preface

The very name *Shakespeare* can overwhelm: so many associations with culture and history. We hope you will approach the plays with curiosity and a willingness to embrace the strangeness of Shakespeare's world: those quaint ways, weapons and words!

Our aim in the **Nelson Thornes Shakespeare** series is to provide a bridge between Shakespeare's world, and our own. For all the differences between the two worlds it is intriguing to find so many similarities: parents and children; power games; loyalty and treachery; prejudice; love and hate; fantasy and reality; comedy and horror; the extremes of human behaviour. It is oddly moving to find that the concerns of the human race have not changed so much over the centuries, and that Shakespeare's themes are modern and recognisable.

The unfamiliarity of the language is best regarded not as a barrier, but as a source of interest. On the left-hand pages we have not only explained unfamiliar words, but have also drawn attention to aspects of wordplay, imagery and verse. The left-hand pages also have reminders that this is a piece of theatre, written to be performed and experienced visually. The **performance features** boxes invite you to consider such questions as: *How might this character react? What actions might be appropriate here? Try reading/acting this section in this way...* You are not fed one interpretation; you make the decisions.

To help you place individual scenes in the context of the whole play there is a **comparison feature** at the end of each scene: *Where else have we seen characters behaving like this? How do events in this scene parallel events two scenes back?* A brief **scene summary** brings together the main developments within that scene.

At the beginning of the play there are some **introductory essays** on background topics. They highlight aspects of Shakespeare's world which show a different outlook to our own: *How did they conduct courtship in his day? How has the status of the monarchy changed? What about their view of magic and the supernatural?*

A separate **Teacher Resource Book** contains material which will help deepen your understanding of the play. There are **worksheets** on individual scenes – valuable if you have missed any of the class study. They will also provide a good background which will help you demonstrate your knowledge in coursework essays. To this end, the book also contains some **Coursework Assignment essay titles** and hints on how to tackle them. The play and resource book together provide enough support to allow you to study independently, and to select the assignment you want to do, rather than all working together as a class.

Our aim is that you finish the play enthused and intrigued, and eager to explore more of Shakespeare's works. We hope you will begin to see that although ideally the plays are experienced in performance, there is also a place for reading together and discussing as a class, or for simply reading them privately to yourself.

Foreword

Who bothers to read introductions, especially introductions to plays by Shakespeare?

Well, you do, obviously, and that's a good start if you want to get more from your literature study. Reading this Foreword will help you to get more from Shakespeare's writing and from the accompanying material provided with the play.

Shakespeare – the great adapter

Shakespeare is regarded as a great writer but not because he was an original inventor of stories. His plays are nearly all adaptations of stories he found in books, or in history – or in somebody else's play. His originality came from the way he used this material. He changed his sources to suit himself and his audiences and was never afraid to change the facts if they didn't suit him.

The best way of understanding what Shakespeare thought valuable in a story is to look at the way he altered what he found.

The **Introductory essays** show how he changed characters or time-scales to enhance the dramatic effect or to suit a small cast of actors.

Shakespeare – the great realist

What Shakespeare added to his source material was his insight into people and society. He understood what makes people tick and what makes society hold together or fall apart. He showed how people behave – and why – by showing their motives and their reactions to experiences such as love, loss, dreams, fears, threats and doubts. These have not changed, even if we think science and technology make us different from people in Shakespeare's day. He was also realistic. He avoided stereotypes, preferring to show people as a complex mixture of changing emotions.

When you use the character sheets provided by your teacher, you will see this realism in action. His characters behave differently in different circumstances, and they change over time – just as we do in real life.

Shakespeare – the language magician

Shakespeare's cleverness with language is not just his ability to write beautiful poetry. He also wrote amusing dialogue, common slang, rude insults and the thoughts of people under pressure. He wrote script that uses the sounds of words to convey emotion, and the associations of words to create vivid images in our heads.

When you use the glossary notes you will see how his language expresses ugliness, hatred, suspicion, doubt and fear as well as happiness, beauty and joy.

Shakespeare – the theatrical innovator

Theatre before Shakespeare was different from today. Ordinary people enjoyed songs and simple shows, and educated people – the minority – enjoyed stories from Latin and Greek. Moral and religious drama taught right and wrong and there were spectacular masques full of music and dance for the audience to join in. Shakespeare put many of these elements together, so most people could expect something to appeal to them. He was a comprehensive writer for a comprehensive audience, writing to please the educated and the uneducated. He was the first to put realistic people from every walk of life on stage – not just kings and generals, but characters who talked and behaved like the ordinary folk in the audience. He was less interested in right and wrong than in the comedy or tragedy of what people actually do. *Only Fools and Horses*, and *EastEnders*, are dramas which follow a trend started by Shakespeare over four hundred years ago. He managed this in theatres which lacked lighting, sound amplification, scene changes, curtains or a large cast of actors.

The performance features accompanying the play text will help to show you how Shakespeare's stagecraft is used to best dramatic effect.

Whether you are studying for GCSE or AS, the examination is designed to test your ability to respond to the following:

1   Shakespeare's ideas and themes
2   Shakespeare's use of language
3   Shakespeare's skill in writing for stage performance
4   The social, cultural and historical aspects of his plays
5   Different interpretations of the plays.

1a. Showing personalities (ideas and themes)

Shakespeare thought drama should do more than preach simple moral lessons. He thought it should show life as it was, daft and serious, joyful and painful. He didn't believe in simple versions of good and evil, heroes and villains. He thought most heroes had unpleasant parts to their nature, just as most villains had good parts. This is why he showed people as a mixture. In *Hamlet*, he wrote that the dramatist should **hold a mirror up to nature**, so that all of us can see ourselves reflected. As he picks on the parts of human behaviour that don't change (fear, jealousy, doubt, self-pity), his characters remind us of people we know today – and of ourselves – not just people who lived a long time ago. This is because Shakespeare shows us more than his characters' status in life. He knew that beneath the robes or the crown there is a heart the same as any tradesman's or poor person's. He knew that nobody in real life is perfect – so he didn't put perfect characters on his stage.

Shakespeare understood that human beings are fickle and not always true to themselves. He shows the comic aspect of this in Benedick's mockery of love and lovers, then his radical transformation into the very kind of love-behaviour he had so recently despised.

1b. Showing what society was/is like (ideas and themes)

In *Hamlet*, Shakespeare declared that drama should show the **form and pressure of the age**, meaning the structure of the times we live in and the pressures and influences it creates.

Elizabethan England had known great conflict and turmoil through civil unrest and was also always under threat from other countries (Shakespeare was 20 at the time of the Spanish Armada). It was also a nation changing from the old ways of country living. London and other cities were growing, and voyagers were exploring other lands. New trades were developing, and plague and disease spread quickly in crowded parts of the cities. Most people were superstitious, but science was beginning to make its mark. People still generally believed in the Divine Right of Kings, but they were beginning to think that bad kings may be removed for the country's good. One such example was Charles I who was executed only 33 years after Shakespeare's death.

The wealthy characters in *Much Ado About Nothing* are excessively concerned with their honour and status. Claudio, for example, is too willing to believe the worst about Hero because he thinks her (assumed) unfaithfulness will make him look foolish.

Concern for status is shown in both the high-class characters and the lower-class characters. Dogberry and Verges are in constant competition for the limelight, each imagining that he is more competent than the other.

2. Shakespeare's use of the English language (sound and image)

Shakespeare wrote the speech of uneducated servants and traders but he could also write great speeches using rhetoric. Whether it is a dim-witted inn-servant called Francis in *Henry IV Part One*, or a subtle political operator like Mark Antony in *Julius Caesar*, Shakespeare finds words to make them sound and seem convincing.

One of Shakespeare's talents was for creating vivid images by linking ideas with familiar experiences. He uses common terms from sports and trades to tap into the audience's own knowledge. For example, when Claudio and Leonato plan to trap Benedick into falling in love with Beatrice, they refer to **stalking** him, a term used in hunting, and they refer to Benedick as the sitting **fowl**. Later, when Hero and Margaret are pulling the same trick on Beatrice, they refer to her as **like a lapwing**, meaning a bird that moves close to the ground to conceal itself. These references may not make too much sense to today's audience, but Shakespeare thought most of his audience would be familiar with the sport of wildfowling.

As in so many other plays, Shakespeare delights in the comedy of language, particularly when language gets mangled in the mouth of a confused or pretentious speaker. Dogberry's inability to find the right word or the right pronunciation is all the more amusing because he believes that he is sounding impressive and superior; this is despite his mixing up of such words as *assembly* and *dissembly*, *comprehended* and *apprehended*, *odorous* and *odious*, *senseless* and *sensible*, *tolerable* and *intolerable*, and *recovered* and *discovered*.

3a. Writing for a mixed audience (writing for stage performance)

As a popular dramatist who made his money by appealing to the widest range of people, Shakespeare knew that some of his audience would be literate, and some not. So he made sure that there was something for everybody – something clever and something vulgar, something comic and something tragic.

Desperate deeds of devilish villainy, comic behaviour of the incompetent Watch and romantic interest provide something for everybody. If the play is a comic entertainment which amusingly shows how there can be much fuss about something trivial, it can also be a warning about the dangers of getting trivial things out of proportion.

3b. Shakespeare's craft (writing for stage performance)

Shakespeare worked with very basic stage technology but, as a former actor, he knew how to give his actors the guidance they needed. His scripts use embedded prompts, either to actors, or to the audience, so that he did not have to write stage directions for his actors. If an actor says, **Put your cap to its proper purpose**, it is a cue to another actor to be using his hat for fancy gestures, rather than wearing it on his head. If an actor comes on stage and says, **So this is the forest of Arden**, we know where the scene is set, without expensive props and scenery.

4. Social, cultural and historical aspects

There are two ways of approaching this. One way is to look at what the plays reveal for us about life in Shakespeare's time – and how it is different from today. The other is to look at what the plays reveal for us about life in Shakespeare's time – and how it is the same today.

Although a comedy, this play touches on the damage and distress caused by the belief that a woman's marriage-value is dependent on virginity. Shakespeare was writing at a time when such things mattered greatly, and family honour could be destroyed by a woman's loose behaviour – though the same thing was not true for men. This raises the issue of how much things have changed in the society of today, and whether they have changed for the better. The play also shows the power of sub-cultures where Benedick, at the start, sees himself as footloose and fancy free, enjoying young male company and despising people who want to settle down and live with one woman. Again, you can ask yourselves whether these are familiar aspects of male behaviour today, or whether they belong to the Elizabethan age.

Enjoy Shakespeare's play! It's your play, too!

Peter Thomas

Introductory essays

1 Women in a man's world

In our society today we take it for granted that men and women are different but have equal rights and abilities. Anti-discrimination laws and equal opportunity policies have removed the old unfairness which made a 'man's world'. Within the home there may still be differences based on gender, such as who does the cooking, who looks after the children and who cleans the bathroom, but legally and in public, life for women has changed for the better.

In our own time the roles played by men and women in the home and the workplace are still keenly debated: should a woman's main responsibility be to her family or her job; is it acceptable for a man to be a 'house husband' and look after the home and children; does the 'new man' of the twenty-first century share the chores equally with the woman if they are both working…?

Today individual choices allow a wide range of solutions to these issues. In Shakespeare's day – in theory at least – there was no debate. Before Shakespeare was born, women had a very different status in public and in private. Then, it was a man's world, and men were keen to keep it that way. Even during Shakespeare's lifetime, this was reflected in every part of life. Thus when King James I in his first speech to Parliament spoke of his authority to rule he said: 'I am the husband, and all the whole isle is my lawful wife; I am the head and it is my body' (C. H. McIlwain [ed.] *The Political Works of James I*, 1918, 272).

James I saw himself as the nation's 'husband'; in other speeches he represented himself as the 'father' of the nation. Both analogies take it for granted that the family and the country were similar because they were ruled by a man.

King James's predecessor Queen Elizabeth I was, of course, a woman – but this was not something planned or wished for. She became Queen only because there were no male heirs to the throne. Her father, King Henry VIII, had married five times in order to try to produce a male heir and many thought that England was seriously weakened by having a woman as its monarch.

Women and the Bible

The view that men should rule over women was accepted at the time partly because it seemed to be supported by the Bible story of Adam who was the first to be created by God. Eve depended on Adam for her very existence since she was made by God from one of Adam's ribs.

The Bible story of the Fall was also used to support the idea of male dominance and female weakness. Adam had wanted to obey God's order not to touch the fruit of the Tree of Knowledge but Eve had tempted Adam to disobey God's command and so mankind was banished from Paradise. The story seemed to justify a view of women as being responsible for all the evils of the world:

> She [Eve] was no sooner made but straightway her mind was set upon mischief, for by her aspiring mind and wanton will she quickly procur'd man's fall. And therefore ever since they are and have been a woe unto man...
>
> Joseph Swetnam, *The Arraignment of Lewd, Idle, Froward and Unconstant Women*, 1615

Men found it useful to exploit this stereotype and represented women as promiscuous, nagging and untrustworthy. Signs of intelligence and independence in women were therefore seen as dangerous faults because they might challenge men's authority.

Women and society

Another factor which supported the view of male dominance was the fear of social disorder. During the fifteenth century the bloody civil war between the houses of York and Lancaster had produced political chaos. Shakespeare, too, lived in troubled and uncertain times. The Wars of the Roses (named after the red rose emblem of Lancaster and the white rose emblem of York) were still in the relatively recent past and resulted in the crown being passed from king to king by bloody warfare and dethronement. Queen Elizabeth I never married so there was no obvious heir to the throne. Religious differences between Protestants and Catholics threatened unrest and rebellion. There were social tensions, too, which brought civil unrest and from abroad there was the constant fear of invasion, particularly from Spain.

It is natural perhaps that in such troubled times there should have been an emphasis on the need to respect authority which meant, in effect, 'obedience' – the subject to obey the monarch, the wife her husband, children their father.

Women and the family

Because men in those days took the view that women were assumed to be both physically and morally inferior to men it was also assumed that when they married they exchanged their labour within the partnership for promises of love and protection. In Shakespeare's *The Taming of the Shrew*, Katherina, the Shrew of the title, eventually accepts that a husband is:

> ...one who cares for thee,
> And for thy maintenance; commits his body
> To painful labour both by sea and land,
> To watch the night in storms, the day in cold,
> Whilst thou liest warm at home, secure and safe;
> And craves no other tribute at thy hands
> But love, fair looks, and true obedience...
>
> *The Taming of the Shrew* Act 5 Scene 2

Since women were by nature promiscuous and could not be trusted to be sexually faithful to their husbands, we can understand the numerous cuckolding jokes in *Much Ado About Nothing* and Benedick's early reluctance to marry. Women who showed intelligence and independence like Beatrice were said to be 'curst' while those who talked too much were 'shrews' or 'scolds'. Shakespeare, however, was too clever to accept the crude sexist stereotype and showed in many of his plays that women could be wiser and more honest than men. He good-humouredly exposes the folly of such stereotypes. However, society had not caught up with Shakespeare's more enlightened views and women who broke the rules could be cruelly punished. 'Scolds' could be brutally gagged with a metal bridle or forcibly ducked underwater on a 'ducking stool'. Communities might also resort to unofficial action to show their disapproval of a woman who beat her husband or had been unfaithful. The 'skimmington ride' (named after the skimming ladle used in the dairy) involved the parading of an effigy of the victim on horseback through the streets accompanied by the banging of pots and pans and cat-calls. Needless to say, there were no corresponding punishments for men, though the skimmington ride humiliated the husband no less than the wife because he was shown to have no authority over his own wife.

In order to preserve male authority, men emphasised other qualities in creating their idea of the ideal woman. Chastity, silence and obedience were encouraged as the traditional female virtues. In *Much Ado About Nothing* Hero, of course, represents these qualities. One of the ways in which Shakespeare challenges social norms is to show that actually possessing these qualities does not prevent Hero from being shamed and humiliated and may even be the cause of injustice and unhappiness.

Women and the law

Married women had fewer rights and less status in common law than unmarried ones. Technically a wife's possessions were the property of her husband, including whatever assets she had brought into the marriage. She did not even have the right to make her own will, though pre-marital settlements could offer some financial protection.

In *The Taming of the Shrew* Petruchio says of his wife, Katherina:

> I will be master of what is mine own.
> She is my goods, my chattels, she is my house,
> My household stuff, my field, my barn,
> My horse, my ox, my ass, my any thing...
>
> *The Taming of the Shrew* Act 3 Scene 2

Petruchio is expressing the conventional view of a man's right to exercise total authority over his wife; she becomes essentially his 'property'. In the play his wife – the 'Shrew' – is brought to submission by a brutal process of starvation, humiliation and sleep deprivation.

Women's changing role

In reality, however, a woman's lot was not always as desperate as this might suggest. About fifteen years after Shakespeare's *The Taming of the Shrew* was performed the playwright John Fletcher wrote a sequel, *The Woman's Prize; or The Tamer Tamed* (1611?) in which the tables are turned on the tyrannical Petruchio by his second wife, Maria. She makes the following observation:

> Tell me of due obedience? What's a husband?
> What are we married for, to carry sumpters [i.e. saddle-bags]
> Are we not one peece with you, and as worthy
> Our own intentions, as you yours?
>
> John Fletcher, *The Woman's Prize; or The Tamer Tamed* Act 3 Scene 3

It seems that women were no longer prepared to be completely subservient. In this they were encouraged by a new view of marriage encouraged by the Protestant Church which emphasised that wives should be treated with consideration and affection, as helpmates and companions rather than obedient servants.

In practice, of course, women had never been as totally under the thumb of their husbands as the law or Shakespeare's play had suggested. Among the upper classes where women had leisure to pursue their own interests, education and accomplishments were considered assets. Lower down the social scale, too, a husband depended on his wife's goodwill and co-operation, and upon her skills in buying and selling at market. An historian from the Netherlands neatly summed up this discrepancy between theory and practice:

> Wives in England are entirely in the power of their husbands,
> their lives only excepted...yet they are not kept so strictly as
> they are in Spain or elsewhere. Nor are they shut up, but they
> have the free management of the house or housekeeping... .
> They go to market to buy what they like best to eat. They are
> well dressed, fond of taking it easy and commonly leave the care
> of household matters and drudgery to their servants...and all
> this with the permission and knowledge of their husbands, as
> such is the custom... . This is why England is called the paradise
> of married women. Van Meteren, *Nederlandsche Historie*, 1575

The law and social convention may have decreed that women should be subservient to men but common sense and the practicalities of day-to-day living usually resulted in a more balanced division of privileges and responsibilities.

2 Wooing and wiving

If we are to understand love and marriage in the age of Shakespeare we shall have to set aside some of our modern ideas and attitudes.

First, it is important to remember that the idea of 'marrying for love' is quite a modern one. In Shakespeare's time both romantic love and sexual attraction were often seen as a poor basis for an effective marriage. They were both likely to make a man forget that marriage should provide him with financial security (i.e. a dowry) and a worthy partner.

Francis Bacon put it like this:

> The stage is more beholding to love than the life of man. For as
> to the stage, love is ever matter of comedies, and now and then
> of tragedies; but in life it doth much mischief; ...it was well
> said, 'That it is impossible to love and be wise'.
> Francis Bacon, *Essayes*, 1597–1625

It is also often assumed – partly because in Shakespeare's *Romeo and Juliet* Juliet is formally wooed at fourteen and the young lovers marry in their mid-teens – that in Shakespeare's time couples married much younger than we do today. They did not. It is true that betrothals could be arranged as young as seven but a marriage could not be consummated until twelve (for girls) and fourteen (for boys). Even so, such marriages were extremely rare. In fact, the average age for marriage was the mid-twenties though the aristocracy and upper gentry – the class of most of the main characters in *Much Ado About Nothing* – tended to marry earlier.

Marriage and the Church

For the Catholic Church virginity and celibacy were the ideal and were a legal obligation for all priests, monks and nuns. The sexual act itself was regarded by the Church as sinful. However, since, in Benedick's words, 'the world must be peopled' (Act 2 Scene 3 line 188) the Church was prepared to accept marriage as a necessary evil – but one that should be moderated by sexual self-control even within marriage.

With the reform of the Catholic Church in the sixteenth century and the gradual emergence of the Protestant Church it came to be recognised that marriage was ordained for mankind by God – a recognition summed up in the idea of 'holy matrimony' – and that love-making could be seen as 'one of the most proper and essential acts of marriage' (William Gouge, *Domesticall Duties*, 1622) because it both produced children and made couples 'dearer to each other's souls' (William Whateley, *A Bride Bush*, 1623). The 1549 Prayer Book saw marriage in terms of 'mutual society, help and comfort, that the one ought to have of the other, both in prosperity and adversity' and the Puritan preacher William Perkins described marriage as 'a state in itself far more excellent than the condition of a single life' (*Christian Economy*, 1595). In this changed climate 'chastity' was no longer identified with refraining from sex but rather with faithful wedded love.

Marriage and property

So far as the law was concerned, marriage was a way of ensuring that property would be passed on by the production and rearing of legitimate children. In *Much Ado About Nothing* Don John is illegitimate, the result of an extra-marital relationship. His jealous and discontented attempts to cause trouble – he is even referred to as 'John the Bastard' – reinforce the traditional warnings against sex outside marriage.

Marriage brought two families and their property together and with this combined wealth came greater influence over public events. The grander the family, the more direct influence parents expected to have over their children's choice of marriage partner. When Juliet in *Romeo and Juliet* defies her father's wishes later in the play he violently abuses and disowns her, and when Hero is thought to have 'shamed' the family Leonato treats her with similar brutality.

For the propertied classes the safeguarding of money, land, influence and status were important but even here enforced marriages were rare and compatibility – a 'companionate' marriage – generally mattered more than either purely romantic or economic considerations. Juliet's father, for example, makes it clear to Paris who asks his permission to marry Juliet that 'My will to her consent is but a part…' (Act 1 Scene 2). At the same time, a man who checked on his love's inheritance prospects even as he declared his admiration for her beauty and virtues was simply being practical and sensible. For Claudio the fact that Hero is her father's only child is vitally important. She has no brother to inherit Leonato's property.

In England, brides who – unlike Hero – were not landed heiresses were unable to bring landed property to a marriage since all land was normally inherited by the eldest son. Instead they were expected to bring a large sum in cash as a dowry or 'portion'.

This money went not to the groom but to his father who often used it himself as a dowry to marry off one of his own daughters. In return the groom's father guaranteed the bride an annuity (called a 'jointure') if she should become a widow. Thus negotiations about dowries and marriage portions among the property-owning classes were routine and parental approval was seen as vital when marriage was a family issue rather than one of personal choice.

The value of virginity

While the Church gradually came to adopt a more enlightened idea of love and marriage, from a practical social standpoint a woman was regarded as a more valuable prospect if she was a virgin. A woman's sexuality was something to be bartered and, at the appropriate time, sold. Late Elizabethan drama is full of jokes about virgins who had hung on to their virginity until its 'currency' was devalued – a woman had to know when to trade it in. Inevitably if virginity was seen as a marketable asset it was more cherished among the upper classes with more property to dispose of.

Modern readers may think this idea not very different from prostitution but we should remember that for most women marriage – or entering a nunnery – was the only 'career' open to them; in practice it was virtually impossible for a woman to remain unmarried and independent. They were thus forced to resort to the means available to them, and virginity was the one form of power that women could exert over men:

> **An unchaste woman lost her value on the marriage market; and if already married, she might corrupt the pure line of descent by insinuating a bastard into it. Consequently a young virgin was counselled to live before her marriage in an utterly chaste manner.** Margaret Loftus Ranald, *Shakespeare and His Social Context*, 1986

In Shakespeare's plays references to a woman's virginity are often couched in terms of material value such as 'chaste treasure' or 'precious jewel'. When Benedick considers the qualities he would require in a woman it is essential that she should be **virtuous** [i.e. a virgin], **or I'll never cheapen her** (Act 2 Scene 3 lines 23–4). In other words, a woman who had lost her virginity was less valuable. Claudio's rejection of Hero because he perceived her to be 'tainted' merchandise is perfectly consistent with this view. At the same time, although pre-marital sex was limited by both social and moral pressures many formally engaged couples anticipated marriage, even in the 'best' families. When Claudio begins his rejection of Hero during the wedding ceremony Leonato assumes that it is Claudio himself who has **made defeat of her virginity** (Act 4 Scene 1 line 42). If so, their being betrothed would apparently have been enough to **extenuate the 'forehand sin** (Act 4 Scene 1 line 45).

Romance and reality

Since marriage was so closely connected with economic considerations and often had little to do with what we understand by 'romantic love', when a man spoke of 'love' he was often merely playing the role of lover expected by custom, a role that was seen as a necessary part of the ritual of courtship. Interestingly, we still use the word 'courting' to describe this stylised form of wooing according to the manners of the 'court'. The courtly wooer was expected to conform to certain conventions of dress, give love tokens (Claudio gives Hero gloves), and use artificial 'poetic' language and music to declare his love. Benedick scorns the fact that Claudio shows a new interest in fashionable clothes once he falls in love but Benedick himself eventually conforms to the stereotype, changing his appearance, putting on perfume and make-up and attempting to write love poetry. In reality, of course, such conventions were often a means of sweetening what was essentially a business transaction. In *Much Ado About Nothing* Claudio woos Hero through the agency of Don Pedro, dowry negotiations with her father take place discreetly off-stage and the couple never even speak before their betrothal. When Claudio believes Hero to be dead and promises that he will marry her 'cousin', without even seeing her, his agreement is obtained with the additionally tempting knowledge that **she alone is heir** to both Leonato and his brother (Act 5 Scene 1 line 253).

At the beginning of this essay we read Francis Bacon's claim that the subject of love was more 'beholding' to the stage than to 'the life of man'. Perhaps audiences enjoyed the idea of romantic love so much in the theatre because it was a luxury they could rarely afford in real life.

3 Formalities and festivities

The various stages of the story of *Much Ado About Nothing* are marked by a variety of communal events, some joyous, others solemn: the arrival of the Prince and his companions to stay at Leonato's house; the masked party to celebrate the visit; the preparations for the wedding of Hero and Claudio and part of the ceremony itself; the solemn ritual of penance at Hero's 'tomb'; the ceremonial betrothal of Claudio to Hero's supposed 'cousin'; and, of course, the dance with which the play ends.

Entertaining VIPs

In some ways Don Pedro's visit to Leonato's estate resembles the 'Progresses' so beloved of Queen Elizabeth herself. These involved her travelling around her realm with an enormous retinue of retainers both to see and be seen by her subjects and staying – sometimes for weeks at a time – in the houses and at the expense of the nobility and the wealthy. It was one way in which the Queen could remind her high-

Queen Elizabeth in procession.

born subjects of who was really in charge. Don Pedro's visit to Leonato is made in a spirit of friendship, but we should not forget that Leonato is the Governor of Messina and that Messina was ruled at the time by Spain. Don Pedro of Arragon represents the ruling nation and so there is also an unspoken 'political' dimension to his visit too.

Entertaining the Queen was regarded by some of the aristocracy as a burden and some avoided the court altogether, living quietly in the country and keeping out of the limelight. The expense was certainly enormous. Sir William Cecil, whose house she visited twelve times during her reign, calculated it cost him two or three thousand pounds a visit – a huge sum in sixteenth-century terms. In *Much Ado About Nothing* the Prince speaks of not wanting to disappoint Leonato because of the **great preparation** made by his host to entertain him. Borachio has been employed as a **perfumer** to sweeten the atmosphere of the rooms for the guests by burning scented wood; Act 1 Scene 2 shows Leonato bustling about organising final arrangements to entertain the Prince and there is mention of the **great supper**.

Of course, many noblemen welcomed the opportunity to entertain the Queen in the hope of winning her favour and bettering themselves. Robert Dudley, Earl of Leicester, staged the most elaborate entertainments for the Queen at Kenilworth in Warwickshire in 1575. These included fireworks, hunting, morris dancing, bear-baiting, an Italian acrobat, a play performed by actors from Coventry and a pageant on the lake with floating islands and an eighteen-foot (5.5 metres) long mermaid. In *Much Ado About Nothing*, of course, the masked ball with its music, elaborate costumes, dancing and general festive atmosphere occupies the stage for many minutes and provides the occasion for a wealth of bawdy humour, disguise and high-spirited practical jokes.

Robert Dudley's elaborate entertainments for the Queen at Kenilworth were all commissioned in hope of the ultimate royal favour – marriage with the Queen. In our play, too, Leonato believes for a time that the Prince intends to propose marriage to his daughter, Hero. This would have been welcomed by Leonato as bringing a considerable step up the social ladder. He tells his daughter: **…if the Prince do solicit you in that kind, you know your answer** (Act 2 Scene 1 lines 48–9).

The masked dance arranged by Leonato for Don Pedro and his entourage (Act 2 Scene 1) resembles the masques that were so popular in the Elizabethan and Stuart courts. Masques began as costume balls designed around a theme; costumed guests would perform a dance before the host and company, after which they would invite the spectators to join them. Typically, masques were occasions for revelling during festive events such as weddings, or at Christmas time. They usually began after supper, continuing into the night and sometimes into early morning.

Marriage rituals

Love, courting and, ultimately, marriage are recurring themes in *Much Ado About Nothing*. It was actually illegal to represent a wedding ceremony on a stage – even if the disruption of the ceremony were not part of the plot – but we can sense something of the excitement of the occasion as Hero seeks advice from her ladies-in-waiting in choosing her wedding dress in Act 3 Scene 4 and in the general atmosphere of sexual banter.

Weddings, like baptisms, usually took place on Sundays and were traditionally celebrated in the church porch. The ceremony would be followed by a wedding sermon in which the minister discoursed solemnly on the responsibilities of marriage. After the wedding ceremony the rest of the day – and often several succeeding days – would be given up to merry-making, beginning with the bridal procession escorted by a band of musicians. The young couple would be showered with gifts of money, plate and linen to help them set up house but there was no 'honeymoon' and precious little privacy, for the high spot of the jollity of every wedding feast was the public 'bedding' of the bride and groom.

It was the bridesmaids' duty to prepare the bride for bed before the groom arrived surrounded by his friends. At grand weddings there might be a bishop to bless the marriage bed but in all cases everyone crowded into the nuptial chamber to offer good wishes, encouragement and explicit advice. One can imagine what sort of an ordeal this must have been for a young and inexperienced couple who, in view of the formal and ritualised courting practices of the time, often barely knew each other.

Among the well-to-do a wedding, marking the hopeful beginning of a new generation, was always a joyous occasion, especially if it represented a step up in the world. Hero may not have married the Prince, Don Pedro, but Claudio was a 'Count' and therefore Leonato would have been well pleased with the match.

Death and salvation

Death was a much more familiar visitor to the Elizabethan home than in our own time and death, like birth and marriage, was an occasion for ceremonial. The departed would be prepared for burial by his or her nearest kin, while the funeral itself was always as elaborate and dignified as the family could afford. A splendid memorial was considered almost as important as a splendid funeral, as the many which still survive readily testify. A young girl would be accompanied to her last resting place by an escort of virgins and her 'maiden garland' hung up in the parish church. In numerous productions of *Much Ado About Nothing* such garlands have been laid during Claudio's ritual penance in Act 5 Scene 3.

The formalities and festivities we have been speaking of so far have all marked essentially social events – entertaining, marriage, death – but the play's treatment of the character of Hero also recalls another annual cycle of festivals experienced by Shakespeare's audiences as part of the Church year. These commemorated important stages in the life of Christ: Christmas when Christ was born, Lent marking the forty days Christ spent in the wilderness and during which he fasted and was tempted by the devil, and Easter when Christ rose from the dead after his crucifixion. These 'rhythms' in the Church calendar would have been as familiar to every citizen as the yearly cycle of the seasons in the natural world.

Shakespeare's audiences were used to a pattern of life regulated by the Church in which moments of celebration alternated with periods of self-denial; in *Much Ado About Nothing* they saw a story which contained certain echoes of this pattern. The masked party brings to mind the Shrovetide carnival celebrations that traditionally came before the period of Lent leading up to Easter. It is during this carnival, of course, that Hero is wooed and joyfully betrothed. Although Hero certainly does not 'represent' the figure of Christ her actual innocence, betrayal and public humiliation all recall something of his sufferings. It is a man of God – the Friar – who devises a plan in which she must **die to live**, a process which brings to mind Christ's resurrection. We witness her 'death' being commemorated and a life that **lives in death** being celebrated. Finally we share in the joy of her 'rebirth': **One Hero died defiled, but I do live** (Act 5 Scene 4 line 63).

In conclusion we should remember that the Elizabethans worked hard and long – the idea of taking a summer holiday as we do would have astonished them – but they played hard too. They made the most of the opportunities for enjoyment offered by a year broken up by religious festivals and outings, fairs and markets as well as occasional family events that were also communal celebrations. A play, too, is a shared experience; an audience takes part in a communal event and Shakespeare knew how to make the most of his audience's eagerness to become involved. The customs and ceremonies they saw represented on stage were also a part of their own lives; through them his audience saw the world of the play as one they could recognise and understand.

4 Valour, honour and the *duello*

The words **honour** and **honorable** occur many times during *Much Ado About Nothing*. For a woman, of course – and for Hero in particular – the word refers specifically to her virginity and sexual faithfulness. For men the meaning of the word was rather different. To the Elizabethan audience, Count Claudio's 'noble' birthright alone would initially guarantee respect but honour could be lost if it was not maintained or if the gentleman's good name became stained. When Don John first describes Hero's supposed infidelity he is quick to remind Claudio of the consequences to his reputation of marrying a woman proved to be disloyal: **…it would better fit your honour to change your mind** (Act 3 Scene 2 lines 82–3).

Honour in war

For a man his reputation in the eyes of others – particularly his peer group – was inextricably linked with his personal courage in feats of arms. In the military action against Don John the youthful Claudio has enhanced his reputation enormously: **He hath borne himself beyond the promise of his age, doing in the figure of a lamb the feats of a lion** (Act 1 Scene 1 lines 11–12). Nowhere is this link between male honour and physical courage more apparent than in Benedick's challenging Claudio to a duel in defence of Hero's honour.

A Prince – the word 'Prince' refers to any ruler, king or queen – historically owed his authority to his prowess in battle. Niccolò Machiavelli makes an even bolder claim:

> **A prince ... should have no other object, no other thought, no other subject of study, than war, its rules and disciplines; this is the only art for a man who commands ...**
>
> Niccolò Machiavelli, *The Prince*, 1513

In 1588 When Queen Elizabeth addressed her land forces gathered at Tilbury to repel the Spanish Armada she admitted that she was physically 'a weak and feeble woman' but she claimed for herself 'the heart and stomach of a king, and of a king of England too…'. Many of Elizabeth's subjects believed that the nation itself was weakened by having a woman as its 'Prince' but on this occasion the Queen arrived at Tilbury on a white steed and wearing a silver cuirass (body armour) as if to demonstrate the 'kingly' virtue of courage. Elizabeth actually retired to safety before the Spanish arrived but what is significant is that she tried to *appear* courageous; she was careful to fashion for herself the image of a brave king.

The equating of honour and military prowess was by no means confined to the role of the monarch. In fact, no idea of masculinity in early modern England was so enduring as the need to display and maintain a reputation for valour, whether it was on the battlefield or in private quarrels. It was the basis of the masculine concept of 'honour'.

Thomas Trussell was typical in claiming that the very idea of 'nobility' and a nobleman's rank derived from prowess in feats of arms:

> **Their honour that they so much glory in, and are so much lifted up with-all, whence had it beginning, or how did their Ancestors attaine unto it? Even by the exercise of Armes, the most honorable titles being bestowed upon the most deserving.**
>
> Thomas Trussell, *The Soldier Pleading His Owne Cause*, 1619

Honour challenged

Warfare and military achievement linked to the idea of male honour are ever-present factors in *Much Ado About Nothing*. The conflict between the illegitimate Don John and his brother that precedes the start of the play is a reminder that struggles for power between members of the same royal family were not uncommon. The play is full of references to swords and bucklers, pikes, scabbards, lances and poniards, and the bantering camaraderie between

Benedick, Don Pedro and Claudio illustrates the close bonds of friendship forged in an exclusively male military culture.

Of course, Shakespeare also pokes fun at these same values. In the first scene of the play news of the action against Don John overlaps with the introduction of the **merry war** between Beatrice and Benedick. Beatrice pokes fun at Benedick's courage and promises to **eat all of his killing** (Act 1 Scene 1 line 33) on the assumption that he won't have killed anyone. According to Beatrice the only challenge that Benedick is fit for would be against Cupid, the child god of love, and she says that Benedick is 'valiant' only in his capacity for eating!

The wooing of Beatrice and Benedick, too, is carried out in a way that can be compared to warring. The war of words and exchanges of wit between the 'lovers' recalls the thrusts and parries of swordplay. On one occasion such is the effectiveness of Beatrice's attacks that Benedick claims to feel like a human target **with a whole army shooting at me** and he goes on to complain that **She speaks poniards** [i.e. daggers] **and every word stabs** (Act 2 Scene 1 line 186). The trick played by their friends on Beatrice and Benedick also resembles a military campaign with manoeuvres and sieges to bring the lovers together and ending in a notable victory when they are betrothed. Now that the serious military action against Don John is won their military instincts must be content with bettering the archer, Cupid, to become **the only love-gods** (Act 2 Scene 1 lines 285–6).

Of course, Beatrice's light-hearted mockery of Benedick's courage turns to contemptuous scorn at the decline of the male military code of honour when her cousin, Hero, is slandered and disgraced: **...manhood is melted into curtsies, valour into compliment, and men are only turned into tongue...** (Act 4 Scene 1 lines 301–2) – in other words, men are all talk! Three times she wishes **O that I were a man!** For Benedick there is only one way to prove his love for Beatrice and redeem both his own honour and that of the male sex: he must challenge Claudio to a duel.

Honour defended – the duel

According to the rules of the duel (from the Italian *duello*) each man of noble or gentle birth was charged with maintaining his honour at all cost. But why did the

A duel in Germany in 1547.

Elizabethan gentleman value honour and reputation so highly? The only socially acceptable ambition in life for a gentleman was to gain noble rank by winning the favour of his Sovereign. Only a few out of hundreds of gentlemen in each generation would attain this ambition so the competition was fierce. Duelling provided each gentleman with a means to demonstrate his skill and courage, prove his willingness to die for noble ideals, and dissuade anyone from disparaging his other virtues:

> **For these and such like offenses the law can make no adequate retribution – in such a state life is a burden, which cannot be laid down or supported, till death either terminates his own existence or that of the despoiler of his peace and honor.**
>
> Quoted in Robert Baldick, *The Duel,* 1965

One important custom was that a duel ended any dispute, and further combat over that issue was forbidden. Another aspect of the Code was that no man of sound body could refuse a challenge without being publicly proclaimed a coward. In *Much Ado About Nothing* Benedick says he will **subscribe him** [Claudio] **a coward** if he fails to answer Benedick's challenge (Act 5 Scene 2 line 41). A person who was challenged to a duel would select the time, place and weapons to be used. Each combatant would choose a second, a person to observe that no treachery or foul play was committed.

Of course, in the play misunderstandings are eventually resolved and the duel proves unnecessary; the deadly challenge can be laughed off with manly posturing threats of **beating** and **cudgelling** (Act 5 Scene 4 lines 100–108). It is particularly appropriate for *Much Ado About Nothing* that the words 'honour' and 'humour' so closely resemble each other. When the **merry war** turns serious Benedick is forced by Beatrice to choose between his allegiance to his male comrades and his loyalty to her. Benedick courageously follows his conscience, not a code, and grows in moral stature while his military friends remain firmly in their old male world, cracking their tired cuckolding jokes to the end.

5 Crime and punishment

The fear of civil war remained strong long after the Wars of the Roses; there were threats of religious strife, a Spanish invasion, and a growing number of unemployed poor. It is hardly surprising that Elizabethans were unusually concerned with preserving order in their society. At the same time Elizabethans constantly lived – in the words of Christopher Marlowe, the dramatist – on 'the slicing edge' of death and were consequently always aware of the fragility of life. Death might claim them at any time, by disease for which there was no cure, by accident, in childbirth or in a casual quarrel on the street which could lead to a drawn knife or sword. Marlowe himself died from a dagger wound above the right eye during a pub brawl.

Elizabethan England – particularly London – was troubled by increasing levels of crime and its society was as violent as our own: quarrels and resentments might be settled by blows and sometimes fights to the death. A matter of honour might well be settled among the upper classes by the *duello* in the same way that Benedick challenges Claudio in *Much Ado About Nothing*. The larger towns were prone to street riots, often started by apprentices and directed against foreigners or other unpopular groups – Shakespeare's society knew about racial discrimination.

'The idle', 'rogues and vagabonds' were feared as carriers of disease and threats to good order and were widely flogged and driven out of the parish – one of the few arrests that Dogberry instructs the Watch to make is to **comprehend** [i.e. apprehend] **all vagrom** [i.e. vagrant] **men** (Act 3 Scene 3 line 18). Certain areas outside the city walls, notably Clerkenwell, were notorious for their brothels and with brothels came bribery, pimps and protection rackets. There was a large mobile population, particularly in times of economic hardship: runaway apprentices, soldiers returning from the wars, evicted tenants and pedlars and beggars all added to a widespread fear of crime and disorder.

One contemporary commentator recorded:

> **Certes there is no greater mischief done in England than by robberies, the first by young shifting gentlemen, which oftentimes do bear more port [i.e. live to a higher standard] than they are able to maintain. Secondly by serving men, whose wages cannot suffice so much as to find them breeches... . Our third annoyers of the commonwealth are rogues, which do very great mischief in all places where they become... .**
>
> William Harrison, *Description of England*, 1587

Just as crime drama is a popular form of entertainment on TV and film today, in Shakespeare's time criminal activity, both in London and on the roads, quickly became a popular subject with the authors of pamphlets and satires as well as dramatists. As writers liked to remind their readers, familiarising yourself with rogues and their tricks was one way to protect yourself against them. Exposés such as John Awdeley's *Fraternity of Vagabonds* (1561) and Thomas Harman's *Caveat for Common Cursetors* (1567) gave detailed descriptions of the activities of what amounted to an alternative society of the road. Other pamphleteers and dramatists like Thomas Dekker and Robert Greene represented London as an urban jungle. Much of this was nothing more than sensationalised fantasy but people were afraid of crime and looked for others to blame. Foreigners and social misfits were easy targets.

Everyday policing was carried out by petty constables, unpaid volunteers like Dogberry and Verges in *Much Ado About Nothing,* whose local knowledge helped them in their task. Shakespeare undoubtedly stereotypes his constables for maximum comic effect, though tradition has it that the character of Dogberry was based on a real constable who lived at Grendon in Buckinghamshire through which Shakespeare would have passed on his way from Stratford-upon-Avon in Warwickshire to London. Unlike Dogberry, however, many constables were literate and were prepared to use their common sense in preventing minor offenders from reaching the courts where punishments were unreasonably harsh. Nevertheless, Shakespeare's creations are clearly based on reality, as this extract reveals:

> [A Constable] is a viceroy in the street, and no man stands
> more upon't than he that he is the king's officer.... He is never
> so much in his majesty as in his night-watch, where he sits in
> his chair of state, a shop-stall, and, environed with a guard of
> halberds, examines all passengers. He is a very careful man in
> his office, but if he stay up after midnight you shall take him
> napping. John Earle, *Micro-cosmographie*, 1628

This picture of the constable being 'never so much in his majesty' fits perfectly with Shakespeare's comic creation of Dogberry. He is a man with a huge ego, full of self-importance and very conscious of the dignity of his position. He is comic, of course, because he is totally unfitted for the job he takes so much pride in. He is totally ignorant of the law and its processes and his instructions to the Watch in Act 3 Scene 3 suggest that his main object is to avoid any trouble. It is a wonderful comic irony that this totally incompetent Watch should bring the truth of Don John's plot to light and ensure that the play finally resolves itself as a comedy rather than a tragedy.

Justices of the Peace – usually selected from the local gentry – conducted the trial and punishment of minor criminals, rather as Leonato deals with the criminals apprehended by the Watch in *Much Ado About Nothing*. They were unpaid and had to cope with the increasing amounts of petty crime, duties which must have encroached considerably upon their private lives. In 1596 a Somerset Justice, Edward Hext, wrote complaining of 'the infinite number of the wicked wandering idle people of the land', idlers who refused to work and poisoned the minds of the decent poor, encouraging them 'to all contempt both of noblemen and gentlemen, continually buzzing into their ears that the rich men have gotten all into their hands and will starve the poor' (*Tudor Economic Documents*, ii, 431).

Punishments were varied and sometimes appear arbitrarily severe to us. Rogues and vagabonds were often put in the stocks and whipped and sometimes burnt through the ears; sheep-stealers could have their hands cut off; 'such as kill by poison are either scalded to death in lead or seething waters' while heretics and witches were burnt at the stake. Criminals guilty of serious crimes like murder, manslaughter and piracy could expect to be hanged but so could all 'felons' – and 'felony' covered a wide range of crimes deemed to be capital offences. These included '…hunting by night with painted faces and visors; rape, or stealing of women and maidens; conspiracy against the person of the prince…; carrying of horses or mares into Scotland; sodomy and buggery; stealing of hawks' eggs…' and so on! Today an accused person has the right to silence but no such right existed in Shakespeare's day:

> Such felons as stand mute...are pressed to death by huge
> weights laid upon a board that lieth over their breast, and a
> sharp stone under their backs, and these commonly hold their
> peace thereby to save their goods unto their wives and children,
> which, if they were condemned, should be confiscated to the
> prince. William Harrison, *Description of England*, 1587

This last brutal punishment reminds us that the torture of prisoners to extract confessions and information was common in Elizabeth's reign, especially in cases of espionage. The England of Elizabeth was a nation under threat, both from factions within and great powers without, particularly Spain. Opposition to the Protestant establishment from Catholics at home and abroad meant that the Queen and her court constantly believed themselves under threat from plots and subterfuge. In this fragile climate, spies and spy networks were of fundamental importance; kidnapping, surveillance, conspiracy and counter-espionage were methods routinely employed to defeat the ever-present threat of regicide – and any method, however cruel, could be justified to preserve the stability of the state. The Gunpowder Plot of 1605 – still remembered today in Guy Fawkes' effigies, bonfires and fireworks – was a Catholic plot devised just two years after Elizabeth I's death to blow up both King James I and his parliament. For those found guilty of such crimes against the state (i.e. treason) was reserved the most terrible punishment of all:

> **That you be drawn on a hurdle to the place of execution where you shall be hanged by the neck and being alive cut down, your privy members [i.e. genitals) shall be cut off and your bowels taken out and burned before you, your head severed from your body and your body divided into four quarters to be disposed of at the King's pleasure.**

By comparison members of the nobility merely had their heads chopped off – a relatively merciful fate.

Finally, it is worth remembering that spying and the propagation of mis-information play an important part in *Much Ado About Nothing*; hanging, drawing and quartering, burning at the stake and crushing by weights are all the subject of jokes during the play and the dance which celebrates the play's conventional 'happy ending' of a double marriage is set against the **brave punishments** being devised for Don John by the amiable Benedick.

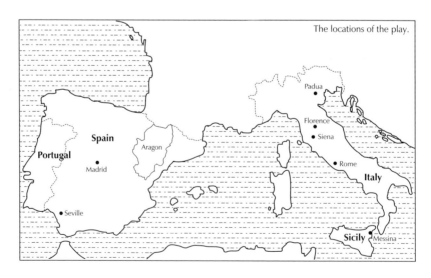

The locations of the play.

The characters

DON PEDRO, Prince of Arragon

CLAUDIO, of Florence
BENEDICK, of Padua } young lords accompanying Don Pedro

DON JOHN, Don Pedro's illegitimate brother (sometimes called the Bastard)

BORACHIO
CONRADE } followers of Don John

LEONATO, Governor of Messina
ANTONIO, his elderly brother
HERO, Leonato's daughter

MARGARET
URSULA } attendants on Hero
BEATRICE, Leonato's niece, an orphan

BALTHASAR, a singer
FRIAR FRANCIS, a priest

DOGBERRY, the Constable in charge of the Watch
VERGES, the Headborough, Dogberry's partner
A Sexton and several Watchmen
A Boy, servant to Benedick
Antonio's son, Musicians and Attendants of Leonato's Household
Other lords attending on Don Pedro, Messengers

1:1

Governor Leonato welcomes Prince Don Pedro and his followers. The opening skirmishes between Beatrice and Benedick give way to Claudio's admission of love Hero, and the Prince's promise to help him woo her.

The play is set in Messina, a seaport in Sicily.

s.d. MESSENGER a member of Leonato's court or a junior officer in Don Pedro's army

1 *Don Pedro of Arragon* Arragon is a province in Spain which ruled Sicily at the time.

3 *by this* by this time. *three leagues* roughly 9 miles or 14 kilometres

5 *gentlemen* men of rank. *have you lost* have been killed on your side. *action* battle, military campaign

6 *any sort* any kind. *name* social rank or reputation

7 *victory is twice itself* winning a war is doubly gratifying

7–8 *full numbers* i.e. there are few fatalities

8 *I find here* Leonato returns to reading the letter. *bestowed much honour* praised greatly

10 *remembered* rewarded or acknowledged

11 *borne himself beyond the promise of his age* behaved more bravely than could have been expected of one so young

12–13 *better bettered expectation* more richly surpassed what could be expected

14 *He hath an uncle here in Messina* the uncle is not referred to again in the play.

16–17 *joy could not … badge of bitterness* His uncle's happiness was unbounded so that he couldn't prevent himself from weeping.

20 *kind* natural. *kindness* human sympathy

Leonato's daughter, Hero, is on stage from the beginning of the scene and exits with the other characters at line 118 – yet she never says a word! What is she doing while she is on stage and where: sitting, standing, painting, gardening? Is she oblivious to what is going on or watching and listening? Is Hero aware of Claudio's love for her at this stage?

23 *Signor Montanto* Beatrice mockingly refers to Benedick. A *montanto* was a fencing thrust.

25 *sort* rank

26 *What* Who. *ask for* enquire about

29 *set up his bills* put up public notices or advertisements

29–30 *challenged Cupid at the flight* challenged Cupid to a long-distance archery contest. Cupid was the Roman god of love represented as a child who shot arrows indiscriminately (he was blind) and whose victims instantly fell in love.

30 *my uncle's fool* Leonato's court fool paid as an in-house entertainer. *subscribed for Cupid* accepted the challenge on Cupid's behalf

31 *challenged him at the birdbolt* since Benedick had offered the challenge,

the fool (acting for Cupid) would have a choice of weapons. A *birdbolt* was a short, blunt arrow suitable for children – and fools.

31–3 *how many hath he killed … his killing* A bragging soldier would claim to eat those he killed in battle. Beatrice doesn't expect Benedick to have killed anyone.

34 *tax* mock, ridicule

34–5 *be meet with you* get even with you. Leonato also puns on meet/meat.

37 *musty victual* stale or mouldy food. *holp* helped

38 *valiant trencher-man* fine eater. A *trencher* was a wooden plate. *excellent stomach* good appetite. The word *stomach* could also refer to both the 'appetites' in general – including sexual appetite – and physical courage.

1:1   *Enter* LEONATO, HERO *and* BEATRICE, *with a* MESSENGER

LEONATO   I learn in this letter that Don Pedro of Arragon comes this night
to Messina.

MESSENGER   He is very near by this; he was not three leagues off when I left
him.

LEONATO   How many gentlemen have you lost in this action?   5

MESSENGER   But few of any sort, and none of name.

LEONATO   A victory is twice itself when the achiever brings home full
numbers. I find here that Don Pedro hath bestowed much honour on a
young Florentine called Claudio.

MESSENGER   Much deserved on his part, and equally remembered by Don Pedro.   10
He hath borne himself beyond the promise of his age, doing in the
figure of a lamb the feats of a lion; he hath indeed better bettered
expectation than you must expect of me to tell you how.

LEONATO   He hath an uncle here in Messina will be very much glad of it.

MESSENGER   I have already delivered him letters, and there appears much joy in   15
him, even so much that joy could not show itself modest enough
without a badge of bitterness.

LEONATO   Did he break out into tears?

MESSENGER   In great measure.

LEONATO   A kind overflow of kindness; there are no faces truer than those   20
that are so washed. How much better is it to weep at joy than to joy at
weeping!

BEATRICE   I pray you, is Signor Montanto returned from the wars, or no?

MESSENGER   I know none of that name, lady; there was none such in the army of
any sort.   25

LEONATO   What is he that you ask for, niece?

HERO   My cousin means Signor Benedick of Padua.

MESSENGER   O, he's returned, and as pleasant as ever he was.

BEATRICE   He set up his bills here in Messina and challenged Cupid at the
flight; and my uncle's fool, reading the challenge, subscribed for Cupid   30
and challenged him at the birdbolt. I pray you, how many hath he killed
and eaten in these wars? But how many hath he killed? For indeed, I
promised to eat all of his killing.

LEONATO   'Faith, niece, you tax Signor Benedick too much; but he'll be meet
with you, I doubt it not.   35

MESSENGER   He hath done good service, lady, in these wars.

BEATRICE   You had musty victual, and he hath holp to eat it; he is a very
valiant trencher-man, he hath an excellent stomach.

MESSENGER   And a good soldier too, lady.

40 *a good soldier to a lady* a ladies' man

41 *A lord to a lord, a man to a man* The messenger is defending Benedick, suggesting that he is a true gentleman. *stuffed* crammed

43–4 *But for the stuffing – well, we are all mortal.* Beatrice doubts whether Benedick is crammed with *honourable virtues* but then admits that no human being is perfect.

48–9 *five wits* the five mental qualities which distinguished human beings from animals: Common Wit, Imagination, Fantasy, Estimation, Memory

49 *halting* limping. *governed with* controlled by

50 *wit enough to keep himself warm* a proverbial expression referring to common sense

50–1 *bear it for a difference* keep it as a way of distinguishing between

51–2 *it is all the wealth … reasonable creature* his one remaining wit is the only way of identifying him as a rational human being rather than an animal

53 *sworn brother* a friendship bound by a solemn oath

56 *next block* a block was the wooden mould on which hats were shaped. Beatrice is suggesting that Benedick's friendships are as changeable as the fashions.

57 *is not in your books* doesn't have your good opinion. We still have the expression 'to be in someone's good (or bad) books'.

58 *an if.* *study* library

59 *squarer* brawler, i.e. someone 'squaring up' for a fight

59–60 *make a voyage with him to the devil?* go with him as his companion to Hell?

63 *pestilence* plague. *presently* immediately

64 *caught the Benedick* Beatrice turns Benedick's name into a disease which produces madness.

65 *thousand pound* Beatrice refers to the greed of the medical profession. *'a* he

66 *hold* keep, stay

69 *not till a hot January* i.e. never

s.d. *Flourish* A fanfare (of horns, trumpets, etc.) to announce the approach of a person of high rank

---

Don Pedro is the most highly ranking character in the play.

How would you stage the entry of the Prince and his officers:

- *marching troops, military band, trumpets and drums?*
- *military banners, festive bunting, flowers?*
- *crowd of local onlookers, cheering, bustle and noise?*
- *as a more low-key affair, welcomed informally by familiar friends?*

s.d. *Don John* Most editions of the play identify Don John as *the Bastard* in the stage directions although his illegitimate birth is not mentioned in the text until Act 4 Scene 1.

71 *are you come to meet your trouble?* Don Pedro is being conventionally polite in acknowledging that his visit will cause *trouble* to his host.

72 *cost* trouble, expense. *encounter* come to meet

73 *in the likeness of your grace* in the shape of Don Pedro himself

73–5 *For trouble … takes his leave* Leonato returns the compliment by suggesting that Don Pedro's arrival dispels trouble and happiness leaves his house only when Don Pedro himself departs.

76 *charge* responsibilities, expense

76–7 *I think this is your daughter?* This is the first reference to Hero in the play. Notice that she says nothing during this long opening scene.

BEATRICE	And a good soldier to a lady. But what is he to a lord?	**40**

MESSENGER A lord to a lord, a man to a man, stuffed with all honourable virtues.

BEATRICE It is so indeed; he is no less than a stuffed man. But for the stuffing – well, we are all mortal.

LEONATO You must not, sir, mistake my niece. There is a kind of merry war **45**
betwixt Signor Benedick and her; they never meet but there's a skirmish of wit between them.

BEATRICE Alas, he gets nothing by that. In our last conflict four of his five wits went halting off, and now is the whole man governed with one; so that if he have wit enough to keep himself warm, let him bear it for a **50** difference between himself and his horse – for it is all the wealth that he hath left, to be known a reasonable creature. Who is his companion now? He hath every month a new sworn brother.

MESSENGER Is't possible?

BEATRICE Very easily possible. He wears his faith but as the fashion of his **55** hat; it ever changes with the next block.

MESSENGER I see, lady, the gentleman is not in your books.

BEATRICE No; an he were, I would burn my study. But I pray you, who is his companion? Is there no young squarer now that will make a voyage with him to the devil? **60**

MESSENGER He is most in the company of the right noble Claudio.

BEATRICE O Lord, he will hang upon him like a disease. He is sooner caught than the pestilence, and the taker runs presently mad. God help the noble Claudio! If he have caught the Benedick, it will cost him a thousand pound ere 'a be cured. **65**

MESSENGER I will hold friends with you, lady.

BEATRICE Do, good friend.

LEONATO You will never run mad, niece.

BEATRICE No, not till a hot January.

MESSENGER Don Pedro is approached. **70**

Flourish. Enter **DON PEDRO, CLAUDIO, BENEDICK, BALTHASAR** *and* **DON JOHN**

DON PEDRO Good Signor Leonato, are you come to meet your trouble? The fashion of the world is to avoid cost, and you encounter it.

LEONATO Never came trouble to my house in the likeness of your grace. For trouble being gone, comfort should remain; but when you depart from me, sorrow abides and happiness takes his leave. **75**

DON PEDRO You embrace your charge too willingly. I think this is your daughter?

LEONATO Her mother hath many times told me so.

BENEDICK Were you in doubt, sir, that you asked her?

80   *for then were you a child* Leonato suggests that he had no need to question his wife's faithfulness since Benedick was only a child and in no position to lead her astray.

81   *You have it full* You are well answered

81–2   *we may guess … being a man* we can estimate from Leonato's words what sort of reputation you now have (i.e. as a womaniser)

82   *fathers herself* Hero's resemblance to Leonato is enough to confirm him as her father.

87   *marks* takes notice of

88   *Lady Disdain* Benedick represents Beatrice as the very embodiment of Scorn or Contempt.

89   *meet* suitable, appropriate (with a pun on 'meat')

90   *Courtesy* Good manners. *convert* change

92   *turncoat* traitor. *of* by

93   *would* wish

95   *dear happiness* great good fortune

96   *pernicious suitor* wicked lover

96–7   *I am of your humour for that* I have the same disposition as you in that respect

99   *still in that mind* always of that opinion. *so* or

100   *'scape* escape. *predestinate* inevitable (i.e. because of Beatrice's bad temper)

103   *rare parrot-teacher* i.e. Beatrice would make a good parrot teacher because she talks the sort of pointless phrases that a parrot might learn.

105–6   *so good a continuer* had as much staying power (as you have in talking)

106   *keep your way* carry on talking. *a'* in. *done* finished

107   *jade's trick* the trick of an awkward horse (which might craftily slip its head out of its collar). Beatrice implies that Benedick has slipped out of this skirmish of wit because he was getting the worst of the contest.

Try speaking Beatrice's line:

You always end with a jade's trick; I know you of old.

- *aloud for all the characters on stage to hear; directly to Benedick so that only he hears; privately, expressing her thoughts to herself*
- *mixing these three ways of delivery between the two halves of the line*
- *in various tone(s) of voice: anger, mockery, bitterness, resignation, frustration.*

How do these different readings affect the impact of the line?

108   *the sum of all* a summary of everything. Don Pedro has presumably been giving Leonato an account of the campaign from which he and his companions have just returned.

110–11   *some occasion may detain* something may happen to keep us here

113   *be forsworn* have sworn falsely

115   *I owe you all duty* I am completely at your service

117   *Please it* Will it please

LEONATO   Signor Benedick, no, for then were you a child.   80

DON PEDRO You have it full, Benedick; we may guess by this what you are, being a man. Truly, the lady fathers herself. Be happy, lady, for you are like an honourable father. [*He begins to talk aside to Leonato*]

BENEDICK   If Signor Leonato be her father, she would not have his head on her shoulders for all Messina, as like him as she is.   85

BEATRICE   I wonder that you will still be talking, Signor Benedick; nobody marks you.

BENEDICK   What, my dear Lady Disdain, are you yet living?

BEATRICE   Is it possible disdain should die, while she hath such meet food to feed it as Signor Benedick? Courtesy itself must convert to disdain, if   90 you come in her presence.

BENEDICK   Then is courtesy a turncoat; but it is certain I am loved of all ladies, only you excepted. And I would I could find in my heart that I had not a hard heart, for truly I love none.

BEATRICE   A dear happiness to women; they would else have been troubled   95 with a pernicious suitor! I thank God and my cold blood, I am of your humour for that; I had rather hear my dog bark at a crow than a man swear he loves me.

BENEDICK   God keep your ladyship still in that mind so some gentleman or other shall 'scape a predestinate scratched face!   100

BEATRICE   Scratching could not make it worse, an 'twere such a face as yours were.

BENEDICK   Well, you are a rare parrot-teacher.

BEATRICE   A bird of my tongue is better than a beast of yours.

BENEDICK   I would my horse had the speed of your tongue, and so good a   105 continuer. But keep your way a' God's name, I have done.

BEATRICE   You always end with a jade's trick; I know you of old.

DON PEDRO That is the sum of all, Leonato. [*Aloud*] Signor Claudio and Signor Benedick, my dear friend Leonato hath invited you all. I tell him we shall stay here at the least a month, and he heartily prays some occasion   110 may detain us longer. I dare swear he is no hypocrite, but prays from his heart.

LEONATO   If you swear, my lord, you shall not be forsworn. [*To* DON JOHN] Let me bid you welcome, my lord – being reconciled to the Prince your brother, I owe you all duty.   115

DON JOHN   I thank you. I am not of many words, but I thank you.

LEONATO   Please it your grace lead on?

DON PEDRO Your hand, Leonato; we will go together.

[*Exeunt all but* BENEDICK *and* CLAUDIO

121   *modest* demure, virginal

123–4   *after my custom … their sex* according to my usual practice as someone recognised as a great critic of women

125   *speak in sober judgement* give a serious opinion

126   *i' faith* seriously. *low* short. *brown* sun-tanned (in Shakespeare's time a fair skin was regarded as a mark of beauty in women)

127   *little* thin, skinny

128   *commendation* praise. *afford* give, offer. *other than she is* any different

129   *unhandsome* unattractive, not pretty. Benedick grudgingly admits that Hero is pretty.

133   *Can the world buy such a jewel?* i.e. Hero is too precious to be bought by all the money in the world.

134   *a case to put it into* Benedick makes a bawdy joke. A woman's virginity (and by association, the vagina) was often known as her 'jewel'. *with a sad brow* seriously

135   *play the flouting Jack* mocking rogue. Benedick thinks Claudio might be trying to trick him into giving a serious answer and then ridicule him in a 'laddish' way. *to tell us* expecting us to believe. *Cupid is a good hare-finder* Cupid was blind and would hardly be able to catch the swift-running hare.

136   *Vulcan a rare carpenter* The Roman god of fire, Vulcan, was a blacksmith not a *rare* (i.e. fine) carpenter.

136–7   Benedick, still unsure whether Claudio is joking, wonders how he can be 'in tune' with Claudio's present mood.

137   *go in* join in with

139   *no such matter* nothing of the sort

140   *her cousin* i.e. Beatrice. *an* if. *possessed with a fury* Benedick implies that Beatrice has an awesome temper.

145–6   *In faith … with suspicion?* A husband whose wife had been unfaithful to him was known as a 'cuckold' and was deemed to have horns on his forehead. The cap to cover them was a sign of ridicule.

147   *Go to!* an expression of disbelief. *An thou wilt needs* if you must. *yoke* the collar used to couple two animals together to draw a plough or cart (i.e. a husband being 'yoked' to a wife)

148   *print* imprint or mark (i.e. the cuckold's horns). *sigh away Sundays* A married man would not be as free to enjoy himself on Sundays as a bachelor and would soon find the day tedious.

Claudio is desperately serious about his love for Hero; Benedick is equally frivolous and mocking.

How would you bring out the contrast between them to make the episode amusing? Think about business, stage movement, tone of voice, use of props and use of costume.

153   *charge* order. *on thy allegiance* on your loyalty to me as your lord

155   *mark you this* take note of this (said to Claudio)

156   *that is your grace's part* that should be your lordship's line (as if prompting him in a play)

158   *If this … uttered* If it were true that I am in love then this would be the right answer (i.e. the *short* answer Benedick had promised).

CLAUDIO	Benedick, didst thou note the daughter of Signor Leonato?
BENEDICK	I noted her not, but I looked on her. 120
CLAUDIO	Is she not a modest young lady?
BENEDICK	Do you question me as an honest man should do, for my simple true judgement? Or would you have me speak after my custom, as being a professed tyrant to their sex?
CLAUDIO	No, I pray thee speak in sober judgement. 125
BENEDICK	Why, i' faith, methinks she's too low for a high praise, too brown for a fair praise, and too little for a great praise. Only this commendation I can afford her – that were she other than she is, she were unhandsome; and being no other but as she is, I do not like her.
CLAUDIO	Thou thinkest I am in sport. I pray thee tell me truly how thou 130 likest her.
BENEDICK	Would you buy her, that you inquire after her?
CLAUDIO	Can the world buy such a jewel?
BENEDICK	Yea, and a case to put it into. But speak you this with a sad brow? Or do you play the flouting Jack, to tell us Cupid is a good hare-finder, 135 and Vulcan a rare carpenter? Come, in what key shall a man take you to go in the song?
CLAUDIO	In mine eye she is the sweetest lady that ever I looked on.
BENEDICK	I can see yet without spectacles, and I see no such matter. There's her cousin, an she were not possessed with a fury, exceeds her as much 140 in beauty as the first May doth the last of December. But I hope you have no intent to turn husband, have you?
CLAUDIO	I would scarce trust myself, though I had sworn the contrary, if Hero would be my wife.
BENEDICK	Is't come to this? In faith, hath not the world one man but he will 145 wear his cap with suspicion? Shall I never see a bachelor of threescore again? Go to, i' faith! An thou wilt needs thrust thy neck into a yoke, wear the print of it – and sigh away Sundays. Look, Don Pedro is returned to seek you.

Enter DON PEDRO

DON PEDRO	What secret hath held you here, that you followed not to 150 Leonato's?
BENEDICK	I would your grace would constrain me to tell.
DON PEDRO	I charge thee, on thy allegiance.
BENEDICK	You hear, Count Claudio? I can be secret as a dumb man; I would have you think so. But on my allegiance – mark you this, on my 155 allegiance – he is in love. With who? Now that is your grace's part. Mark how short his answer is – with Hero, Leonato's short daughter.
CLAUDIO	If this were so, so were it uttered.

159 *Like the old tale* It's the familiar story (of someone who is in love yet strongly denies it)

159–60 *'It is not so … should be so.'* Benedick mocks the way that lovers strongly deny being in love and yet *'God forbid it should be so!'* introduces the possibility that it might well be so in the future.

161–2 *God forbid it should be otherwise!* Claudio finally admits his feelings openly.

163 *Amen* So be it.   *worthy* virtuous (and/or of high rank)

164 *to fetch me in* to trick me into revealing my feelings

165 *troth* truth, honour
speak my thought say what I really think

172 *die in it at the stake* Being burnt at the stake was sometimes a punishment for people who held religious beliefs different from those maintained by the Church. Benedick says he will die a heretic to the religion of love.

173 *in the despite of* in contempt of

174 *And never … force of his will.* It is only by a conscious act of will that Benedick can maintain his role (as a mysogynist or woman-hater). Heretics were condemned not for believing but for wilfully and obstinately holding their views. There are also sexual puns on *part* (penis) and *will* (sexual urges).

176 *recheat* a call to hounds played on a hunting horn. Here it refers again to the cuckold's horns.

177 *winded* sounded.   *bugle* i.e. penis.   *baldrick* A leather belt or girdle worn from one shoulder across the chest to hold a sword or bugle. Here the *invisible* 'holder' of the *bugle* is the vagina.

179 *fine* conclusion; penalty for holding his 'heretical' belief

180 *go the finer* fare better or happier

183 *Prove that ever* If you could ever prove that.   *lose more blood with love* a lover's sighs were said to use up his blood, hence his proverbial paleness (see line 181)

183–4 *get again with drinking* drinking was thought to replenish blood

184 *pick out … ballad-maker's pen* lovers were notorious writers of sentimental ballads

184–5 *hang me up … blind Cupid* Most shops had a sign outside to show the nature of their business. Brothels traditionally had a sign depicting Cupid, the god of love.

186 *fall from this faith* change your beliefs, i.e. fall in love

186–7 *a notable argument* a great subject for discussion

188 *bottle* wicker basket. Cats were sometimes barbarously used for archery target practice in this way.

189 *Adam* Probably a reference to an Adam Bell, a famous archer.

190 *as time shall try* time will be the test (of your determination).   *bear the yoke* See line 147.

192 *vilely* crudely, i.e. unskilfully

196 *horn-mad* stark mad (i.e. mad with rage at having been made a cuckold)

197 *quiver* case for holding arrows.   *Venice* Venice had a reputation for loose sexual morals at this time

198 *quake* tremble (also alludes back to *quiver* meaning 'shake')

199 *I look for an earthquake too, then.* Benedick is being ironic; an earthquake is a very rare event.

BENEDICK	Like the old tale, my lord, 'It is not so, nor 'twas not so; but indeed, God forbid it should be so.'	160

CLAUDIO If my passion change not shortly, God forbid it should be otherwise!

DON PEDRO Amen, if you love her, for the lady is very well worthy.

CLAUDIO You speak this to fetch me in, my lord.

DON PEDRO By my troth, I speak my thought. 165

CLAUDIO And in faith, my lord, I spoke mine.

BENEDICK And by my two faiths and troths, my lord, I spoke mine.

CLAUDIO That I love her, I feel.

DON PEDRO That she is worthy, I know.

BENEDICK That I neither feel how she should be loved, nor know how she 170
should be worthy, is the opinion that fire cannot melt out of me; I will
die in it at the stake.

DON PEDRO Thou wast ever an obstinate heretic in the despite of beauty.

CLAUDIO And never could maintain his part but in the force of his will.

BENEDICK That a woman conceived me, I thank her; that she brought me up, 175
I likewise give her most humble thanks. But that I will have a recheat
winded in my forehead, or hang my bugle in an invisible baldrick, all
women shall pardon me. Because I will not do them the wrong to
mistrust any, I will do myself the right to trust none; and the fine is –
for the which I may go the finer – I will live a bachelor. 180

DON PEDRO I shall see thee, ere I die, look pale with love.

BENEDICK With anger, with sickness, or with hunger, my lord; not with love.
Prove that ever I lose more blood with love than I will get again with
drinking, pick out mine eyes with a ballad-maker's pen, and hang me up
at the door of a brothel-house for the sign of blind Cupid. 185

DON PEDRO Well, if ever thou dost fall from this faith, thou wilt prove a notable
argument.

BENEDICK If I do, hang me in a bottle like a cat and shoot at me; and he that
hits me, let him be clapped on the shoulder and called Adam.

DON PEDRO Well, as time shall try. 'In time the savage bull doth bear the yoke.' 190

BENEDICK The savage bull may, but if ever the sensible Benedick bear it, pluck
off the bull's horns, and set them in my forehead. And let me be vilely
painted, and in such great letters as they write, 'Here is good horse to
hire,' let them signify under my sign, 'Here you may see Benedick, the
married man.' 195

CLAUDIO If this should ever happen thou wouldst be horn-mad.

DON PEDRO Nay, if Cupid have not spent all his quiver in Venice, thou wilt
quake for this shortly.

BENEDICK I look for an earthquake too, then.

200 *temporise with the hours* moderate with the passing of time

201 *repair* make your way

203 *matter* common sense. *embassage* mission

203–4 *and so I commit you* a conventional form of farewell

205 *tuition* safe-keeping. Claudio and Don Pedro tease Benedick by supplying phrases suitable for a letter-ending.

206 *sixth of July* Midsummer Day, an ideal date for Midsummer madness

207 *The body of your discourse* the main substance of your conversation

208 *guarded* ornamented, trimmed. *fragments* leftovers. *basted* loosely sewn

209 *flout old ends* mock me with scraps of wit

When Benedick leaves, the scene changes from 'laddish' banter to a more serious tone; this is reflected in the change from prose to blank verse. How could this be represented on stage? Think about:
- the relationship between Claudio and Don Pedro – Prince and subject, military comrades, friends
- differences in age and experience
- the language they use – 'masculine' military words and the softer language of love
- Claudio's motives.

211 *My liege* My lord. *do me good* help me

212 *My love is thine to teach* You only need to tell me what you want in order for me to show my friendship towards you

217 *affect* love

218 *this ended action* the war just over

221 *drive* steer

223 *vacant* empty

225 *prompting* reminding

226 *ere* before

227 *presently* without delay

229 *cherish* treasure

230 *break* bring up the subject

232 *twist so fine a story* tell such an elaborate tale

233 *minister to* look after

234 *complexion* another reference to the paleness of the lover. See line 183.

235 *too sudden seem* might seem to have come about too quickly (and therefore seem insincere)

236 *salved* soothed. *a longer treatise* a more detailed account

237 *flood* river

238 *The fairest grant is the necessity* The greatest benefit is that which satisfies what is required

239 *Look what will serve is fit* Whatever method works is appropriate.
'tis once briefly, once and for all

240 *fit thee with the remedy* provide you with the cure

242 *assume thy part* pretend to be you

Don Pedro Well, you will temporise with the hours. In the meantime, good   200
      Signor Benedick, repair to Leonato's, commend me to him, and tell him
      I will not fail him at supper; for indeed he hath made great preparation.

Benedick   I have almost matter enough in me for such an embassage; and so I
      commit you –

Claudio   To the tuition of God. From my house – if I had it –   205

Don Pedro The sixth of July. Your loving friend, Benedick.

Benedick   Nay, mock not, mock not. The body of your discourse is sometime
      guarded with fragments, and the guards are but slightly basted on
      neither. Ere you flout old ends any further, examine your conscience;
      and so I leave you.   *[Exit*   210

Claudio   My liege, your highness now may do me good.

Don Pedro My love is thine to teach; teach it but how,
      And thou shalt see how apt it is to learn
      Any hard lesson that may do thee good.

Claudio   Hath Leonato any son, my lord?   215

Don Pedro No child but Hero, she's his only heir.
      Dost thou affect her, Claudio?

Claudio   O my lord,
      When you went onward on this ended action,
      I looked upon her with a soldier's eye,
      That liked, but had a rougher task in hand   220
      Than to drive liking to the name of love;
      But now I am returned, and that war-thoughts
      Have left their places vacant, in their rooms
      Come thronging soft and delicate desires,
      All prompting me how fair young Hero is,   225
      Saying I liked her ere I went to wars –

Don Pedro Thou wilt be like a lover presently,
      And tire the hearer with a book of words.
      If thou dost love fair Hero, cherish it,
      And I will break with her and with her father,   230
      And thou shalt have her. Was't not to this end
      That thou began'st to twist so fine a story?

Claudio   How sweetly you do minister to love,
      That know love's grief by his complexion!
      But lest my liking might too sudden seem,   235
      I would have salved it with a longer treatise.

Don Pedro What need the bridge much broader than the flood?
      The fairest grant is the necessity.
      Look what will serve is fit; 'tis once, thou lovest,
      And I will fit thee with the remedy.   240
      I know we shall have revelling tonight.
      I will assume thy part in some disguise,

244 *in her bosom* privately. *unclasp* open up
246 *amorous* passionate
247 *break* See line 230.
249 *presently* See line 63.

The scene ends positively and optimistically, with the Prince assuring Claudio that Hero **shall be thine** (line 248). Everything doesn't go entirely to plan, however – Don Pedro's plan has been overheard by two people. Look out for the reaction of his brother, Don John, in Act 1 Scene 3 and what happens when the plan is put into practice (Act 2 Scene 1).

News of the recent war and the arrival of Don Pedro and his followers give way to the subject of love. Beatrice and Benedick use it to score verbal points off each other; Claudio's admission of his love for Hero exposes him to merciless teasing from Benedick and Don Pedro and confirms Benedick's hostility to marriage. Nevertheless, the Prince offers to help by disguising himself and wooing Hero on Claudio's behalf at the masked party that evening.

1:2

Amid the preparations for the masked party Leonato learns unexpected news. The Prince, it seems, is in love with Hero and intends to propose marriage to her that evening. Hero will be told so that she is not taken by surprise.

This scene is too short for major changes to the setting. How would you suggest on stage the bustle of preparing for the party:
* *food/decorations, musicians, off-stage sound effects, servants, cleaning?*

1 *cousin* kinsman. *your son* The character is never mentioned again after this scene.
6 *As the event stamps them* It depends on the outcome.
they have a good cover on the face of it things look promising
7–8 *thick-pleached alley* a walk bounded by thickly interlaced hedges
9 *discovered* revealed
11 *accordant* in agreement. *take the present time by the top* grasp the opportunity
12 *break with you of it* raise the subject with you
13 *wit* sense, intelligence
15 *appear itself* actually happens
17 *peradventure* by any chance
18–19 *I cry you mercy* I beg your pardon. This probably refers to the musician that Antonio's son was *busy about* in the opening lines.

Hero is to be told by her father that Don Pedro intends to propose to her so that she can be **better prepared for an answer** (lines 16–17). See how she reacts when she learns the truth in Act 2 Scene 1.

---

*In a play that has much to do with listening, 'noting' and eavesdropping, this is the first example of its potential for confusion. The **good sharp fellow** (line 14) who reported Don Pedro's conversation with Claudio has clearly misheard and completely misunderstood the plan.*

And tell fair Hero I am Claudio,
And in her bosom I'll unclasp my heart,
And take her hearing prisoner with the force   245
And strong encounter of my amorous tale.
Then after to her father will I break,
And the conclusion is, she shall be thine.
In practice let us put it presently.

[*Exeunt*

1:2   *Enter* LEONATO *and* ANTONIO

LEONATO   How now, brother? Where is my cousin, your son? Hath he
provided this music?

ANTONIO   He is very busy about it. But, brother, I can tell you strange news
that you yet dreamt not of.

LEONATO   Are they good?   5

ANTONIO   As the event stamps them; but they have a good cover, they show
well outward. The Prince and Count Claudio, walking in a thick-
pleached alley in mine orchard, were thus much overheard by a man of
mine: the Prince discovered to Claudio that he loved my niece your
daughter, and meant to acknowledge it this night in a dance; and if he   10
found her accordant, he meant to take the present time by the top and
instantly break with you of it.

LEONATO   Hath the fellow any wit that told you this?

ANTONIO   A good sharp fellow. I will send for him, and question him yourself.

LEONATO   No, no, we will hold it as a dream till it appear itself. But I will   15
acquaint my daughter withal, that she may be the better prepared for an
answer, if peradventure this be true. Go you and tell her of it.

Enter ATTENDANTS, *led by* ANTONIO'S SON *with* BALTHASAR

Cousins, you know what you have to do. [*To* BALTHASAR] O, I cry you
mercy, friend; go with me and I will use your skill. [*To* ANTONIO'S SON]
Good cousin, have a care this busy time.   20

[*Exeunt*

1:3

Although the illegitimate Don John is supposedly reconciled (Act 1 Scene 1 line 114) with his brother he remains bitter and vindictive. He dismisses Conrade's advice to hide his malice and ill-humour and looks for opportunities for revenge.

*This scene needs a complete change of mood from the bustle and anticipation of the previous scene and the **great supper** (line 30) going on offstage. How could this be managed through:*

- *costume; ominous theme music; off-stage sounds (from the party?); stage lighting (sinister atmosphere)?*

1	*What the good-year* a general oath such as 'What the devil!'. *out of measure* excessively
3	*There is no measure … breeds* There is no limit to the causes of my depression
6	*what blessing brings it?* what good will it do?
7	*present remedy* immediate cure. *patient sufferance* a means of enduring your suffering patiently
8–9	*born under Saturn* Someone born under the influence of the planet Saturn was thought to be likely to have a gloomy or melancholy character.
9	*goest about to* should attempt to
9–10	*to apply … mortifying mischief* to treat an incurable physical disease (his melancholy) with abstract moral principles
11	*stomach* appetite. *wait for no man's leisure* not wait for anybody else
13	*claw no man in his humour* flatter no one in a bad mood
14	*make the full show of this* reveal this aspect of your character
15	*without controlment* freely, openly
16	*newly* recently, once again. *grace* favour
16–18	*where it is … own harvest* i.e. Don John will only prosper and flourish by his own timely efforts.
18	*frame* engineer
19	*canker* the wild or dog-rose. Don John would rather be free than dependent on his brother's favour.
20	*better fits my blood* (1) more suitable for my temperament (2) more suitable because I'm illegitimate. *disdained of all* looked down on by everybody. *fashion a carriage* put on a false demeanour
23	*muzzle* a device worn placed around a dog's mouth to prevent it from biting. *enfranchised* liberated. *clog* a heavy wooden block tied to an animal's leg to prevent it from straying. (Don John is frustrated by what he sees as humiliating restrictions on his freedom.)
24	*decreed* decided. *sing* i.e. be contented. *had my mouth* i.e. wasn't 'muzzled'
28	*I make … use it only* I make full use of it for it's the only aspect of me that I make use of
33	*model* framework
33–4	*What is he for a fool* What kind of fool is he
34	*betroths* gets engaged to be married. *unquietness* worry, anxiety
35	*Marry* A general exclamation (from the expression 'By the Virgin Mary!')
36	*exquisite* wonderful (ironic)
37	*Even he* The very person!
38	*A proper squire!* a fine young gallant or lover (again ironic).

1:3   *Enter Don John and CONRADE his companion*

CONRADE   What the good-year, my lord! Why are you thus out of measure sad?

DON JOHN   There is no measure in the occasion that breeds; therefore the sadness is without limit.

CONRADE   You should hear reason.   5

DON JOHN   And when I have heard it, what blessing brings it?

CONRADE   If not a present remedy, at least a patient sufferance.

DON JOHN   I wonder that thou – being, as thou sayest thou art, born under Saturn – goest about to apply a moral medicine to a mortifying mischief. I cannot hide what I am. I must be sad when I have cause, and smile at   10
no man's jests; eat when I have stomach, and wait for no man's leisure; sleep when I am drowsy, and tend on no man's business; laugh when I am merry, and claw no man in his humour.

CONRADE   Yea, but you must not make the full show of this till you may do it without controlment. You have of late stood out against your brother,   15
and he hath ta'en you newly into his grace, where it is impossible you should take true root but by the fair weather that you make yourself; it is needful that you frame the season for your own harvest.

DON JOHN   I had rather be a canker in a hedge than a rose in his grace, and it better fits my blood to be disdained of all than to fashion a carriage to   20
rob love from any. In this, though I cannot be said to be a flattering honest man, it must not be denied but I am a plain-dealing villain. I am trusted with a muzzle and enfranchised with a clog – therefore I have decreed not to sing in my cage. If I had my mouth, I would bite; if I had my liberty, I would do my liking. In the meantime, let me be that I am,   25
and seek not to alter me.

CONRADE   Can you make no use of your discontent?

DON JOHN   I make all use of it, for I use it only. Who comes here?

Enter BORACHIO

What news, Borachio?

BORACHIO   I came yonder from a great supper. The Prince your brother is   30
royally entertained by Leonato, and I can give you intelligence of an intended marriage.

DON JOHN   Will it serve for any model to build mischief on? What is he for a fool that betroths himself to unquietness?

BORACHIO   Marry, it is your brother's right hand.   35

DON JOHN   Who – the most exquisite Claudio?

BORACHIO   Even he.

DON JOHN   A proper squire! And who? And who? Which way looks he?

Don John.

40 *forward March-chick* precocious young woman (a *March-chick* was a young bird hatched early in the year)
How came you to this? How did you come to hear about this?

41 *entertained* employed
perfumer someone who was employed to deal with unpleasant domestic smells by burning sweet-scented woods
smoking fumigating
musty stale-smelling

42 *hand in hand* side by side
sad conference serious conversation

43 *arras* tapestry, wall hanging

46 *prove food to my displeasure* provide something for my discontent to feed on

47 *start-up* upstart
all the glory of my overthrow We know that Claudio had excelled in the military campaign against Don John (Act 1 Scene 1 lines 10–13).
cross obstruct

48 *sure* reliable, trustworthy

51–2 *that I am subdued* (1) now that I have been defeated (2) when I am in low spirits

52 *a' my mind* had the same outlook as myself
go prove go and try out

54 *wait* attend

*Don John has portrayed himself as a **plain-dealing villain** (line 22). How would you convey his character in (a) his behaviour (b) his delivery of particular lines? For example:*

• *How does he react to Conrade and Borachio – and they to him?*
• *Look in detail at the remarks he makes about Claudio and Hero (lines 30–54). Try speaking the lines aloud. What tone of voice will you use: scornful, sneering, threatening, sinister, mocking?*

Don John is contemptuous of any man who **betroths himself to unquietness** (line 34) by getting married. How do his vews on marriage compare with those of Benedick in Act 1 Scene 1?
The scene ends with Don John hoping to make mischief but not yet knowing how. See how he improvises a plot in Act 2 Scene 1.

The villainous Don John is resentful that Claudio has gained credit for his overthrow and is held in high regard by the Prince, Don Pedro. He is determined to cause trouble. When Borachio brings news of Don Pedro's promise to woo Hero for Claudio, Don John hopes to use this news to get his revenge.

BORACHIO   Marry, on Hero, the daughter and heir of Leonato.

DON JOHN   A very forward March-chick! How came you to this?   **40**

BORACHIO   Being entertained for a perfumer, as I was smoking a musty room, comes me the Prince and Claudio, hand in hand in sad conference. I whipped me behind the arras, and there heard it agreed upon that the Prince should woo Hero for himself, and having obtained her, give her to Count Claudio.   **45**

DON JOHN   Come, come, let us thither. This may prove food to my displeasure. That young start-up hath all the glory of my overthrow – if I can cross him any way, I bless myself every way. You are both sure, and will assist me?

CONRADE   To the death, my lord.   **50**

DON JOHN   Let us to the great supper – their cheer is the greater that I am subdued. Would the cook were a' my mind! Shall we go prove what's to be done?

BORACHIO   We'll wait upon your lordship.

[*Exeunt*

2:1

*The **great supper** is over and the masked dance begins. Beatrice quickly sees through Benedick's disguise and teases him unmercifully. Don John nearly succeeeds in causing a jealous rift between Claudio and the Prince but Hero and Claudio are ultimately betrothed. Don Pedro undertakes to make Beatrice and Benedick fall in love with each other.*

3 *tartly* sour

5 *melancholy* One of the four 'humours'. *Melancholy* arose from a prevalence of black bile.

7 *image* statue

8 *my lady's eldest son* The firstborn son would inherit any title and property and might well be spoilt and indulged. *tattling* chattering, prattling

Why does this scene begin with a conversation about Don John?

- Can the opening lines be made to 'overlap' the end of the previous scene so that Don John is seen exiting at the end of Act 1 Scene 3?
- In one film version Don John grabs the hand of a startled Hero and kisses it. What other stage business could be used to draw attention to him and so prompt the dialogue?

11–12 *a good leg and a good foot … purse* physically well built and wealthy; there is also sexual innuendo in *foot* as a euphemism for 'penis' and *purse* for 'scrotum'.

12 *'a* he

13 *good will* sexual desire. *Will* was a common euphemism for the sexual organs of both sexes.

14 *By my troth* a mild oath used to give emphasis to what follows; *troth* = truth, faithfulness

15 *shrewd* severe, michievous

16 *curst* perverse, cantankerous

17 *lessen God's sending* reduce what God has given me

18 *'God sends a curst cow short horns'* a proverbial saying which suggests that God's world is so perfectly ordered that he ensures that those who are vicious cannot inflict much harm

20 *God will send you no horns* you will never get a husband; *horns* is another symbol for 'penis'

21 *Just* Just so, exactly. *if he send me no husband* Beatrice acknowledges the obvious logic of Antonio's remark but also refers to the familiar horns/cuckold link.

23 *lie in the woollen* sleep between rough blankets (as opposed to smooth sheets)

24 *light on* come across; fall on top of (another sexual pun)
that hath no beard i.e. is not physically mature

29–30 *take sixpence in earnest of the bear-ward, and lead his apes into hell* accept a token payment from the bear-keeper as an advance payment. Bear-baiting was a cruel but popular sport; here it is suggested that the bear-keeper also kept apes for the same purpose. Leading apes into hell was said to be the fate of women who died as virgins.

32–3 *like an old cuckold with horns on his head* The traditional image of the devil having horns provides an obvious connection with the cuckold.

34 *deliver I up* I hand over

35 *Saint Peter* Traditionally Saint Peter is heaven's gatekeeper, admitting the saved.

2:1   *Enter* LEONATO, ANTONIO, HERO, BEATRICE, MARGARET *and* URSULA

LEONATO   Was not Count John here at supper?

ANTONIO   I saw him not.

BEATRICE   How tartly that gentleman looks! I never can see him but I am
heart-burned an hour after.

HERO   He is of a very melancholy disposition.   5

BEATRICE   He were an excellent man that were made just in the mid-way
between him and Benedick – the one is too like an image and says
nothing, and the other too like my lady's eldest son, evermore tattling.

LEONATO   Then half Signor Benedick's tongue in Count John's mouth, and
half Count John's melancholy in Signor Benedick's face –   10

BEATRICE   With a good leg and a good foot, uncle, and money enough in his
purse – such a man would win any woman in the world, if 'a could get
her good will.

LEONATO   By my troth, niece, thou wilt never get thee a husband if thou be so
shrewd of thy tongue.   15

ANTONIO   In faith, she's too curst.

BEATRICE   Too curst is more than curst. I shall lessen God's sending that way,
for it is said, 'God sends a curst cow short horns'; but to a cow too curst
he sends none.

LEONATO   So, by being too curst, God will send you no horns?   20

BEATRICE   Just, if he send me no husband; for the which blessing I am at him
upon my knees every morning and evening. Lord, I could not endure a
husband with a beard on his face – I had rather lie in the woollen!

LEONATO   You may light on a husband that hath no beard.

BEATRICE   What should I do with him? Dress him in my apparel and make   25
him my waiting gentlewoman? He that hath a beard is more than a
youth; and he that hath no beard is less than a man – and he that is
more than a youth is not for me, and he that is less than a man, I am
not for him. Therefore I will even take sixpence in earnest of the bear-
ward, and lead his apes into hell.   30

LEONATO   Well then, go you into hell?

BEATRICE   No, but to the gate; and there will the devil meet me, like an old
cuckold with horns on his head, and say, 'Get you to heaven, Beatrice,
get you to heaven; here's no place for you maids'. So deliver I up my
apes and away to Saint Peter for the heavens. He shows me where the   35
bachelors sit, and there live we as merry as the day is long.

ANTONIO [*To* HERO] Well, niece, I trust you will be ruled by your father.

BEATRICE   Yes, faith, it is my cousin's duty to make curtsy and say, 'Father, as
it please you.' But yet for all that, cousin, let him be a handsome fellow,
or else make another curtsy and say, 'Father, as it please me.'   40

37 *ruled by* instructed by

41 *fitted with* another sexual pun

43 *metal* substance, material. *earth* Of the four elements (Fire, Air, Water, Earth) Earth was the basest

43–4 *Would it not grieve a woman* The Bible says that God made Adam 'of the dust of the ground' (Genesis chapter 2, verse 7) and then made Eve out of one of Adam's ribs. Beatrice thinks that women's orgin is superior to that of men.

44 *over-mastered with* ruled by. *valiant* compacted

45 *make an account of her life* have to justify herself. *clod of wayward marl* a lump of solid clay

46–7 *Adam's sons … kindred* Beatrice says that since we are all Adam's descendants it would be sinful to marry a member of her own family (*kindred*).

48–9 *solicit you in that kind* importune you on the subject of marriage.

50–1 *in good time* early, soon. Beatrice also puns on the regular beat of the *music* (line 50).

51 *too important* too importunate, over-eager. *measure* moderation; the rhythm of the music

52 *dance out the answer* spin out your answer for the whole length of the dance

53 *measure* a stately dance. *cinquepace* a lively dance with five steps followed by a leap

54 *full as fantastical* just as fanciful

55 *mannerly modest* decent and moderate. *ancientry* old formality

56 *cinquepace* pronounced 'sink-a-pace'. Beatrice puns on the idea of marriage 'sinking' faster and faster *till he sink into his grave.*

58 *you apprehend passing shrewdly* you have a sharp understanding

59 *I can see a church by daylight* i.e. she can avoid marriage and can see what's obvious to anyone

60 *Make good room!* Make space (for the dance)

Masking was a favourite pastime in Elizabethan households and the entry of the maskers and musicians would introduce a high-spirited carnival atmosphere. How would you create this mood: masks; carnival costumes; musicians; dancing.
• Does the dialogue take place while the speakers are dancing? Look for clues in the text!

61 *walk about* perhaps simply 'take a walk with' but a *bout* was also a section of a grave and stately dance called the 'pavane'. *friend* also meant 'lover'

62 *say nothing* don't say anything rude. A 'thing' is a common euphemism for the penis; a woman has 'no thing' and *nothing* can therefore refer to the female genitalia.

65 *when I please* when I want to (i.e. when you please me); when you fancy me (i.e. when I please you)

67 *favour* face (Don Pedro is masked); attractiveness. *defend* forbid. *lute* a stringed musical instrument something like a guitar. Don Pedro's *case* (mask) is

clearly grotesque and Hero hopes that the face inside it will be more handsome.

69 *visor* mask. *Philemon's roof … Jove* In Greek mythology, two poor peasants, Philemon and his wife Baucis, offered hospitality in their cottage to Jove, the king of the gods, not realising his identity

70 *thatched* like Philemon's cottage roof; perhaps bearded

71 *Speak low if you speak love* speak softly if you want to speak of love; or, more vulgarly, you will need to talk about things lower than the thatch if you want to discuss love

Apart from her brief comment in line 5 these are the first words that Hero has spoken. At this stage she believes Don Pedro is about to propose to her.
• Is she coy, innocent, knowing, teasing, provocative?
• How should her lines be spoken? Experiment with different readings.

75 *I say my prayers aloud* a sign of the over-zealous religious 'enthusiast'

Leonato [*To* **Beatrice**] Well, niece, I hope to see you one day fitted with a
    husband.

Beatrice   Not till God make men of some other metal than earth! Would it
    not grieve a woman to be over-mastered with a piece of valiant dust? To
    make an account of her life to a clod of wayward marl? No, uncle, I'll   **45**
    none. Adam's sons are my brethren, and truly I hold it a sin to match in
    my kindred.

Leonato   Daughter, remember what I told you – if the Prince do solicit you in
    that kind, you know your answer.

Beatrice   The fault will be in the music, cousin, if you be not wooed in good   **50**
    time. If the Prince be too important, tell him there is measure in
    everything and so dance out the answer. For hear me, Hero: wooing,
    wedding and repenting is as a Scotch jig, a measure and a cinquepace;
    the first suit is hot and hasty like a Scotch jig, and full as fantastical; the
    wedding mannerly modest, as a measure, full of state and ancientry; and   **55**
    then comes repentance and, with his bad legs, falls into the cinquepace
    faster and faster, till he sink into his grave.

Leonato   Cousin, you apprehend passing shrewdly.

Beatrice   I have a good eye, uncle; I can see a church by daylight.

Leonato   The revellers are entering, brother. Make good room! [*He and*   **60**
    Antonio *put on masks*]

        Enter **Don Pedro, Claudio, Benedick, Balthasar, Don John, Borachio**
            and others (masked)

            The dance begins

Don Pedro Lady, will you walk about with your friend?

Hero   So you walk softly and look sweetly and say nothing, I am yours for
    the walk; and especially when I walk away.

Don Pedro With me in your company?

Hero   I may say so, when I please.   **65**

Don Pedro And when please you to say so?

Hero   When I like your favour, for God defend the lute should be like the
    case!

Don Pedro My visor is Philemon's roof; within the house is Jove.

Hero   Why, then your visor should be thatched.   **70**

Don Pedro Speak low if you speak love.

            They move aside

Benedick   Well, I would you did like me.

Margaret   So would not I, for your own sake, for I have many ill qualities.

Benedick   Which is one?

Margaret   I say my prayers aloud.   **75**

77 *match* partner
God match me with a good dancer! Margaret is questioning Benedick's skills both as a dancer and as a potential lover ('dancing' is a euphemism for sexual intercourse).

78 *Amen* So be it. Balthasar has been listening to the conversation between Margaret and Benedick. He suggests he himself could fulfil the roles of both dancing and sexual partner better than Benedick.

79 *And God … dance is done!* Margaret wants to enjoy herself with a one-night stand but doesn't want her lover to hang around afterwards getting serious.

80 *Answer, clerk.* answer 'Amen' as the clerk responds to prayers in church

81 *No more words* Balthasar has heard enough hints from Margaret. As she takes him as her partner in the next stage of the dance he looks forward to deeds rather than words.
is answered has the answer he wants

83 *At a word* in brief

85 *counterfeit* impersonate

86 *do him so ill-well* imitate his failings so convincingly

87 *his dry hand* a sign of old age
up and down completely, entirely

90 *mum* be quiet

90–1 *graces … an end* virtues must reveal themselves, and that's that

96 *disdainful* sneering, scornful
my good wit the best of my witticisms

97 *Hundred Merry Tales* a book of mostly bawdy comic tales published in 1526

98 *What's he?* Who is he? Benedick, like the other male characters, is disguised in a mask, although Beatrice clearly knows who he is.

103 *the Prince's jester, a very dull fool* a jester was an entertainer or fool maintained in a prince's court or nobleman's household. Beatrice taunts Benedick that he plays the role badly.

104 *impossible slanders* improbable insults
libertines debauched, loose-living people

105 *the commendation* the extent to which he is praised
villainy offensiveness

105–6 *he both pleases men and angers them* he amuses them and annoys them (when they are the target of his *slanders*)

107 *in the fleet* in the company
would wish
boarded tackled; *boarded* also has sexual overtones

109 *break a comparison or two* make insulting similes. The image is from jousting where the contestants on horseback charged at each other with lances.
on me about me

110 *peradventure* probably
not marked not noticed

110–11 *strikes him into melancholy* sends him into a depression

111 *there's a partridge wing saved* Beatrice has previously described Benedick as *a very valiant trencher-man* (Act 1 Scene 1 lines 37–8) but when he is sulking he even loses his appetite for a tiny *partridge wing*.
the fool repeats the idea of Benedick's being *the Prince's jester* (line 103)

112 *the leaders* those couples leading the next phase of the dance

BENEDICK	I love you the better – the hearers may cry 'Amen'.	
MARGARET	God match me with a good dancer!	
BALTHASAR	Amen.	
MARGARET	And God keep him out of my sight when the dance is done! Answer, clerk.	80

She changes partners

BALTHASAR	No more words – the clerk is answered!	

They move aside

URSULA	I know you well enough – you are Signor Antonio.	
ANTONIO	At a word, I am not.	
URSULA	I know you by the waggling of your head.	
ANTONIO	To tell you true, I counterfeit him.	85
URSULA	You could never do him so ill-well, unless you were the very man. Here's his dry hand up and down – you are he, you are he.	
ANTONIO	At a word, I am not.	
URSULA	Come, come, do you think I do not know you by your excellent wit? Can virtue hide itself? Go to, mum, you are he; graces will appear and there's an end.	90

They move aside

BEATRICE	Will you not tell me who told you so?	
BENEDICK	No, you shall pardon me.	
BEATRICE	Nor will you not tell me who you are?	
BENEDICK	Not now.	95
BEATRICE	That I was disdainful, and that I had my good wit out of the Hundred Merry Tales – well, this was Signor Benedick that said so.	
BENEDICK	What's he?	
BEATRICE	I am sure you know him well enough.	
BENEDICK	Not I, believe me.	100
BEATRICE	Did he never make you laugh?	
BENEDICK	I pray you, what is he?	
BEATRICE	Why, he is the Prince's jester, a very dull fool – only his gift is in devising impossible slanders. None but libertines delight in him, and the commendation is not in his wit but in his villainy, for he both pleases men and angers them; and then they laugh at him and beat him. I am sure he is in the fleet – I would he had boarded me.	105
BENEDICK	When I know the gentleman, I'll tell him what you say.	
BEATRICE	Do, do. He'll but break a comparison or two on me, which peradventure not marked or not laughed at, strikes him into melancholy; and then there's a partridge wing saved, for the fool will eat no supper that night. We must follow the leaders.	110

114   *the next turning* i.e. in the dance

- *At what point does Beatrice realise that she is speaking to Benedick – or does she know all the time?*
- *How might Benedick try to disguise his voice? Experiment with different accents.*
- *How will the audience be able to enjoy Benedick's reactions as he is teased by Beatrice? Think about the implications of his mask, the characters' relative positions on stage, his gestures and posture, his tone of voice. Try out different readings with and without the face masked.*

115   *amorous on* in love with
withdrawn her father taken her father aside

116   *The ladies follow her* At the end of the dance the men and women dancers leave the stage in separate lines, the ladies led by Hero.

116–17   *one visor remains* Only the men wore masks. Claudio remains on stage.

118–19   *his bearing* the way he stands

122   *very near my brother in his love* a close friend of my brother

123–4   *no equal for his birth* not of the same social rank

124   *do the part of an honest man* i.e. by dissuading him from marrying Hero

128   *banquet* not a main meal but light refreshment after the dance

132   *constant* steady, reliable

133   *Save* except
office business

134   *all hearts … own tongues* all those in love should speak for themselves

136   *agent* mediator

137   *faith melteth into blood* loyalty converts to passion

138   *an accident of hourly proof* an occurrence confirmed repeatedly

139   *mistrusted* suspected

144   *next* nearest
willow a garland of 'weeping' willow symbolised the forsaken lover

145–6   *usurer's chain* Rich merchants often wore a chain around the neck. They were also often *usurers* (money-lenders). Having 'lent' Hero to Don Pedro, Claudio is entitled to charge 'interest'.

146   *a lieutenant's scarf* a lieutenant in the army wore a sash to show his rank. Benedick suggests that Claudio should challenge Don Pedro to a duel.

BENEDICK	In every good thing.
BEATRICE	Nay, if they lead to any ill, I will leave them at the next turning.

Dance

[*Exeunt all, dancing, but* DON JOHN, BORACHIO *and* CLAUDIO

DON JOHN　Sure my brother is amorous on Hero and hath withdrawn her father　**115**
　　　　to break with him about it. The ladies follow her and but one visor
　　　　remains.

BORACHIO [*Aside to* DON JOHN] And that is Claudio – I know him by his
　　　　bearing.

DON JOHN　[*To* CLAUDIO] Are not you Signor Benedick?　　　　**120**

CLAUDIO　You know me well, I am he.

DON JOHN　Signor, you are very near my brother in his love. He is enamoured
　　　　on Hero – I pray you dissuade him from her; she is no equal for his
　　　　birth. You may do the part of an honest man in it.

CLAUDIO　How know you he loves her?　　　　**125**

DON JOHN　I heard him swear his affection.

BORACHIO　So did I too, and he swore he would marry her tonight.

DON JOHN　Come, let us to the banquet.

[*Exeunt, leaving* CLAUDIO *alone*

CLAUDIO　Thus answer I in name of Benedick
　　　　But hear these ill news with the ears of Claudio.　　　　**130**
　　　　'Tis certain so; the Prince woos for himself.
　　　　Friendship is constant in all other things,
　　　　Save in the office and affairs of love.
　　　　Therefore, all hearts in love use their own tongues;
　　　　Let every eye negotiate for itself,　　　　**135**
　　　　And trust no agent – for beauty is a witch
　　　　Against whose charms faith melteth into blood.
　　　　This is an accident of hourly proof,
　　　　Which I mistrusted not. Farewell therefore, Hero.

Enter BENEDICK

BENEDICK　Count Claudio?　　　　**140**

CLAUDIO　Yea, the same.

BENEDICK　Come, will you go with me?

CLAUDIO　Whither?

BENEDICK　Even to the next willow, about your own business, County. What
　　　　fashion will you wear the garland of? About your neck, like an usurer's　**145**
　　　　chain? Or under your arm like a lieutenant's scarf? You must wear it
　　　　one way, for the Prince hath got your Hero.

CLAUDIO　I wish him joy of her.

149 *drovier* cattle dealer. Having sold his cattle the dealer hopes the purchaser will find them satisfactory. *so* that's how

150 *served you thus* treated you this way

152 *you strike like the blind man* you hit out blindly, i.e. you've hit the wrong man

153 *post* messenger

In this exchange between Benedick and Claudio, Benedick's attempts at witty banter are 'thrust aside' by Claudio who believes himself betrayed by Don Pedro. Compare this episode with the one in Act 5 Scene 1 (lines 110-80) when the roles are reversed and it is Benedick's turn to be deadly serious.

155 *sedges* reeds growing near water. The image is of a wounded bird seeking cover from the hunter.

157 *go under that title* have that reputation. *merry* light-hearted

157–8 *but so … myself wrong* but by presuming this to be the case I am too inclined to think badly of myself

158 *I am not so reputed* I don't have that reputation

158–9 *base though bitter disposition* ignoble nature

159 *puts the world into her person* reports her own personal opinion of me as if it were everyone's opinion

162 *Troth* In truth. *Lady Fame* The personification of Rumour, often represented as having many eyes, tongues and ears.

163 *a lodge in a warren* a cottage in the middle of parkland (i.e. isolated, lonely)

163–4 *I told him, and I think I told him true* Benedick clearly does not know of the plan for Don Pedro to woo Hero on Claudio's behalf.

169 *flat transgression* plain foolishness

170 *steals* This was pronounced 'stales' and suggests a pun on 'stale' (prostitute).

171 *Wilt thou make a trust a transgression?* Are you suggesting that trust is a fault?

173 *amiss* inappropriate

175 *bestowed on you* beaten you with. *as I take it* as I understand the situation. There is also a pun on *take* as 'steal'. *his bird's nest* i.e. Hero

176 *teach them to sing* i.e. teach Hero to 'sing in tune' with Claudio's proposal

177 *If their singing answer your saying* if she proves what you say (by responding to Claudio)

179 *wronged by you* wounded by your slanders

180 *block* i.e. of wood

180–1 *but with one green leaf* i.e. barely living

181 *answered her* engaged in debate with her. *my very visor* my mask itself

182–3 *not thinking I had been myself* not realising who I was (Beatrice had known it was Benedick, of course)

183–4 *duller than a great thaw* more dreary than a thaw after snow

184 *huddling* piling. *impossible conveyance* incredible ingenuity

185 *mark* target

186 *poniards* daggers

186–7 *If her breath were as terrible as her terminations* if her breath was as offensive as her words

BENEDICK   Why, that's spoken like an honest drovier; so they sell bullocks. But
did you think the Prince would have served you thus?   **150**

CLAUDIO   I pray you, leave me.

He thrusts him roughly aside

BENEDICK   Ho! Now you strike like the blind man; 'twas the boy that stole
your meat and you'll beat the post.

CLAUDIO   If it will not be, I'll leave you.

[*Exit*

BENEDICK   Alas, poor hurt fowl, now will he creep into sedges. But that my   **155**
Lady Beatrice should know me and not know me – the Prince's fool?
Hah! It may be I go under that title because I am merry. Yea, but so I
am apt to do myself wrong. I am not so reputed. It is the base though
bitter disposition of Beatrice that puts the world into her person, and so
gives me out. Well, I'll be revenged as I may.   **160**

Enter DON PEDRO

DON PEDRO Now, signor, where's the Count? Did you see him?

BENEDICK   Troth, my lord, I have played the part of Lady Fame. I found him
here as melancholy as a lodge in a warren. I told him, and I think I told
him true, that your grace had got the good will of this young lady; and I
offered him my company to a willow tree, either to make him a garland,   **165**
as being forsaken, or to bind him up a rod, as being worthy to be
whipped.

DON PEDRO To be whipped? What's his fault?

BENEDICK   The flat transgression of a schoolboy who, being overjoyed with
finding a bird's nest, shows it his companion, and he steals it.   **170**

DON PEDRO Wilt thou make a trust a transgression? The transgression is in the
stealer.

BENEDICK   Yet it had not been amiss the rod had been made, and the garland
too. For the garland he might have worn himself, and the rod he might
have bestowed on you, who (as I take it) have stolen his bird's nest.   **175**

DON PEDRO I will but teach them to sing and restore them to the owner.

BENEDICK   If their singing answer your saying, by my faith you say honestly.

DON PEDRO The Lady Beatrice hath a quarrel to you – the gentleman that
danced with her told her she is much wronged by you.

BENEDICK   O, she misused me past the endurance of a block! An oak but with   **180**
one green leaf on it would have answered her – my very visor began to
assume life and scold with her. She told me, not thinking I had been
myself, that I was the Prince's jester, that I was duller than a great
thaw; huddling jest upon jest with such impossible conveyance upon
me, that I stood like a man at a mark, with a whole army shooting at   **185**
me. She speaks poniards and every word stabs. If her breath were as
terrible as her terminations, there were no living near her; she would

188–9 *though she were endowed … before he transgressed* even if her dowry was the entire contents of Garden of Eden (i.e. all Creation) before the Fall

189–90 *She would … turned spit* Hercules was the immensely strong hero of Greek legend but turning the spit on which meat was roasted was the most lowly and humiliating of kitchen maids' jobs.

190–1 *and have cleft … fire too* Chopping up Hercules' legendary club for firewood would be similarly humiliating to the hero's masculinity.

191–2 *the infernal Ate* Ate was the hellish goddess of discord and destruction. She was usually represented as dressed in rags.

192 *in good apparel* well dressed

193 *conjure* exorcise. A *scholar* would be necessary to speak the Latin incantations of the exorcism.

194 *sanctuary* religious retreat. *upon purpose* deliberately

194–5 *would go thither* want to go there (i.e. to Hell – to escape from Beatrice)

195 *disquiet* unrest. *perturbation* disorder

198 *slightest* most trivial. *Antipodes* the far end of the world

200 *bring you the length of* measure and report to you.
Prester John a legendary Christian king supposed to have ruled in Asia or Africa

201 *the great Cham* emperor of the Moguls. *embassage* errand
Pigmies Although the actual Pigmy race was not known in Shakespeare's time, tales of a legendary race of dwarfs had long figured in literature.

202 *harpy* a legendary destructive bird in Greek mythology. It had the face of a beautiful woman and the body of a bird with eagle's talons.

205 *a dish* delicacy; it also refers to sexual appeal (we still use the word 'dishy')

205–6 *Lady Tongue* Beatrice is caricatured in terms of her sharp tongue; it also refers back to the *dish* of (usually) calf's tongue.

208 *gave him use for it* returned it with interest (*use* suggests 'usury')

208–9 *a double heart* Each had 'lent' the other his/her heart but Benedick had taken his back again thus having two.

209 *Marry* a mild oath, 'By the Virgin Mary'. *of* from

210 *with false dice* i.e. by cheating

How should Beatrice's speech (lines 208–10) be spoken: with bitterness, regret, wistfully, light-heartedly, tearfully? Does it hint at a previous close relationship between Beatrice and Benedick that came to nothing? Does Beatrice feel cheated and let down? Does it explain the **merry war**? Does it give Don Pedro the idea for his plan to have them marry?

211 *put him down* got the better of him (as in a wrestling contest)

212 *So I would not he should do me* i.e. lay her down for sex

212–13 *the mother of fools* i.e. any children fathered by Benedick, *the Prince's jester* (line 103), would certainly be *fools*

219–20 *civil Count, civil as an orange* puns on civil (i.e. serious) and 'Civill' which was the spelling at that time for Seville in Spain, famous for its oranges

220 *of that jealous complexion* yellow (i.e. the colour of the orange) was associated with jealousy

221 *blazon* description (a term from heraldry)

221–2 *if he be so* i.e. jealous

222 *conceit* notion, idea

infect to the north star. I would not marry her though she were endowed with all that Adam had left him before he transgressed. She would have made Hercules have turned spit, yea and have cleft his club   190
to make the fire too. Come, talk not of her – you shall find her the infernal Ate, in good apparel. I would to God some scholar would conjure her; for certainly, while she is here, a man may live as quiet in hell as in a sanctuary, and people sin upon purpose because they would go thither; so indeed all disquiet, horror, and perturbation follows her.   195

Enter CLAUDIO *and* BEATRICE

DON PEDRO   Look, here she comes.

BENEDICK   Will your grace command me any service to the world's end? I will go on the slightest errand, now, to the Antipodes, that you can devise to send me on. I will fetch you a tooth-picker, now, from the furthest inch of Asia – bring you the length of Prester John's foot – fetch you a hair   200
off the great Cham's beard – do you any embassage to the Pigmies – rather than hold three words' conference with this harpy. You have no employment for me?

DON PEDRO   None, but to desire your good company.

BENEDICK   O God, sir, here's a dish I love not; I cannot endure my Lady   205
Tongue.

[*Exit*

DON PEDRO   Come lady, come, you have lost the heart of Signor Benedick.

BEATRICE   Indeed, my lord, he lent it me a while and I gave him use for it, a double heart for his single one. Marry, once before he won it of me, with false dice; therefore your grace may well say I have lost it.   210

DON PEDRO   You have put him down, lady, you have put him down.

BEATRICE   So I would not he should do me, my lord, lest I should prove the mother of fools. I have brought Count Claudio, whom you sent me to seek.

DON PEDRO   Why, how now, Count – wherefore are you sad?   215

CLAUDIO   Not sad, my lord.

DON PEDRO   How then? Sick?

CLAUDIO   Neither, my lord.

BEATRICE   The Count is neither sad, nor sick, nor merry, nor well, but civil Count, civil as an orange; and something of that jealous complexion.   220

DON PEDRO   I'faith, lady, I think your blazon to be true, though I'll be sworn, if he be so, his conceit is false.

Enter LEONATO *and* HERO

Here, Claudio, I have wooed in thy name and fair Hero is won; I have broke with her father and his good will obtained. Name the day of marriage, and God give thee joy!   225

227   *all Grace* i.e. God

229   *the perfectest herald* the best messenger; i.e. he is so happy that he could not express it in words

231   *dote upon* delight in

232   *stop his mouth* silence him

235   *poor fool* a term of affectionate scorn.
the windy side A sailing ship that manoeuvred to the windward side of an enemy ship would take the wind from the enemy's sails and so have an advantage.

238   *Good Lord for alliance!* Three cheers for marriage! (Beatrice reacts to Claudio's calling her *cousin*. As Hero's husband, Claudio and Beatrice will be related by marriage.).
Thus goes … world i.e. everyone gets married

239   *I am sunburnt* Elizabethans valued a fair skin as a sign of beauty.
'Heigh-ho for a husband' a proverbial expression referring to a woman sighing to be married

241   *I would rather … getting* Beatrice turns the Prince's use of *get* (line 240) into a pun on 'begetting' (i.e. produce a child).

243   *come by* acquire, obtain

247   *no matter* nothing of importance

248   *to be merry best becomes you* you are at your most appealing when you are in high spirits

250   *my mother cried* i.e. with the pain of child-bearing

250–1   *a star danced* Beatrice invents her own bit of astronomy to explain her *merry* disposition.

253   *I cry you mercy* I beg your pardon.
By your grace's pardon She asks the Prince's permission to leave.

What prompts Don Pedro's proposal to Beatrice – and is it a serious one?
- Are lines 238–9 spoken flippantly, emotionally, with regret, with resignation?
- Is the proposal spoken in the hearing of the other characters – or privately?
- Is it accompanied by extravagant gestures – or with quiet sincerity?
- Is Beatrice flattered, embarrassed, moved by his offer?
- Is Don Pedro hurt, amused, offended by her refusal?

Try out different readings and stagings. Which do you prefer?

255   *melancholy element* Like the element Earth the *melancholy* humour was cold and dry. Beatrice has no trace of melancholy in her temperament.

Compare these lines (255–8) with those on the temperaments of Don John and Borachio, Act 1 Scene 3 lines 8–28.

---

260   *mocks … out of suit* ridicules all her suitors out of their intended courtship of her

265   *rites* puns on the ritual of the wedding ceremony and the physical act that will consummate the marriage

LEONATO	Count, take of me my daughter and with her my fortunes. His grace hath made the match and all Grace say Amen to it!
BEATRICE	Speak, Count, 'tis your cue.
CLAUDIO	Silence is the perfectest herald of joy; I were but little happy if I could say how much. Lady, as you are mine, I am yours. I give away myself for you and dote upon the exchange.

230

BEATRICE	Speak, cousin; or, if you cannot, stop his mouth with a kiss and let not him speak neither.
DON PEDRO	In faith, lady, you have a merry heart.
BEATRICE	Yea, my lord, I thank it, poor fool; it keeps on the windy side of care. My cousin tells him in his ear that he is in her heart.

235

CLAUDIO	And so she doth, cousin.
BEATRICE	Good Lord for alliance! Thus goes every one to the world but I, and I am sunburnt; I may sit in a corner and cry 'Heigh-ho for a husband'!
DON PEDRO	Lady Beatrice, I will get you one.

240

BEATRICE	I would rather have one of your father's getting – hath your grace ne'er a brother like you? Your father got excellent husbands, if a maid could come by them.
DON PEDRO	Will you have me, lady?
BEATRICE	No, my lord, unless I might have another for working days; your grace is too costly to wear every day. But I beseech your grace pardon me; I was born to speak all mirth and no matter.

245

DON PEDRO	Your silence most offends me, and to be merry best becomes you; for, out a' question, you were born in a merry hour.
BEATRICE	No, sure, my lord, my mother cried; but then there was a star danced and under that was I born. Cousins, God give you joy!

250

LEONATO	Niece, will you look to those things I told you of?
BEATRICE	I cry you mercy, uncle. By your grace's pardon.

[*Exit*

DON PEDRO	By my troth, a pleasant-spirited lady.
LEONATO	There's little of the melancholy element in her, my lord. She is never sad but when she sleeps, and not ever sad then, for I have heard my daughter say she hath often dreamed of unhappiness and waked herself with laughing.

255

DON PEDRO	She cannot endure to hear tell of a husband?
LEONATO	O, by no means – she mocks all her wooers out of suit.

260

DON PEDRO	She were an excellent wife for Benedick.
LEONATO	O Lord, my lord! If they were but a week married they would talk themselves mad.
DON PEDRO	County Claudio, when mean you to go to church?
CLAUDIO	Tomorrow, my lord. Time goes on crutches till Love have all his rites.

265

49

267	*answer my mind* as I want them
268	*breathing* delay. *warrant* promise
270	*Hercules' labours* According to Greek legend, Hercules had to perform twelve 'labours' or feats of immense difficulty as punishment for killing his wife and children.
272	*fain* wish, desire. *fashion* create
274	*watchings* without sleep
280	*noble strain* good family. *approved valour* demonstrated courage
281	*honesty* honour
283	*practise on* cunningly work upon
283–4	*queasy stomach* becomes easily nauseous (i.e. at the idea of marriage)
284–5	*Cupid … archer* i.e. Cupid will have to surrender his title to them
286	*drift* plan

*Witty exchanges on the subject of marriage give way to revelry and dancing. Don Pedro begins the wooing of Hero, and Beatrice gets the better of Benedick in another instalment of their **merry war**. Claudio is initially taken in by Don John's lies but jealousy turns to joy as Don Pedro confirms that Claudio and Hero will be married. Benedick's feelings have been hurt by Beatrice's earlier remarks but the Prince reveals a plan to turn their usual rivalry to love and marriage.*

2:2

Foiled in his first attempt to ruin Claudio's happiness, Don John now seizes on Borachio's plan to destroy his marriage plans by tricking Claudio into believing that Hero is unfaithful.

Some productions have linked this scene with the previous one to create a sense of continuity and ironic contrast: in one production Don John had witnessed the betrothal of Hero and Claudio from a balcony from where he spoke; in another, Don John entered as Hero and Claudio were exchanging a parting kiss.

In what other ways could you achieve a similar effect: consider the on-stage picture and/or off-stage sound. Could you utilise the carnival debris left over from the previous scene?

3	*bar* obstruction. *medicinable to me* restore me to health
3–4	*I am sick … to him* I am out of favour (i.e. with his brother, Don Pedro) because of him. Compare Act 1 Scene 3 line 47.
4	*comes athwart his affection* thwarts his inclination; *affection* also suggests Claudio's love for Hero as well as the favour in which Claudio is held by Don Pedro
5	*ranges evenly* matches
6	*covertly* cunningly, secretly
6–7	*no dishonesty … in me* I shall not be suspected of any dishonesty
12	*unseasonable instant* unlikely time. *appoint* arrange for

LEONATO   Not till Monday, my dear son, which is hence a just seven-night and
     a time too brief too, to have all things answer my mind.

DON PEDRO Come, you shake the head at so long a breathing, but I warrant
     thee, Claudio, the time shall not go dully by us. I will in the interim
     undertake one of Hercules' labours, which is to bring Signor Benedick   270
     and the Lady Beatrice into a mountain of affection, th'one with th'other.
     I would fain have it a match and I doubt not but to fashion it, if you
     three will but minister such assistance as I shall give you direction.

LEONATO   My lord, I am for you, though it cost me ten nights' watchings.

CLAUDIO   And I, my lord.   275

DON PEDRO And you too, gentle Hero?

HERO   I will do any modest office, my lord, to help my cousin to a good
     husband.

DON PEDRO And Benedick is not the unhopefullest husband that I know. Thus
     far can I praise him: he is of a noble strain, of approved valour and   280
     confirmed honesty. I will teach you how to humour your cousin, that
     she shall fall in love with Benedick; and I, with your two helps, will so
     practise on Benedick that, in despite of his quick wit and his queasy
     stomach, he shall fall in love with Beatrice. If we can do this, Cupid is
     no longer an archer; his glory shall be ours, for we are the only love-   285
     gods! Go in with me, and I will tell you my drift.

                                             [*Exeunt*

2:2   *Enter* DON JOHN *and* BORACHIO

DON JOHN   It is so. The Count Claudio shall marry the daughter of Leonato.

BORACHIO   Yea, my lord; but I can cross it.

DON JOHN   Any bar, any cross, any impediment will be medicinable to me. I am
     sick in displeasure to him, and whatsoever comes athwart his affection
     ranges evenly with mine. How canst thou cross this marriage?   5

BORACHIO   Not honestly, my lord, but so covertly that no dishonesty shall
     appear in me.

DON JOHN   Show me briefly how.

BORACHIO   I think I told your lordship a year since how much I am in the
     favour of Margaret, the waiting gentlewoman to Hero?   10

DON JOHN   I remember.

BORACHIO   I can, at any unseasonable instant of the night, appoint her to look
     out at her lady's chamber window.

14 *What life … this marriage?* How will that help to kill this marriage?

15 *The poison of that lies in you to temper It up* to you to mix effectively the poisonous ingredients (i.e. of jealousy and suspicion); *temper* = blend together in proper proportions

17–18 *whose estimation … hold up* of whose respect you must declare your own high opinion

18 *contaminated* impure; perhaps diseased. *stale* whore

20 *misuse* deceive. *vex* torment. *undo* ruin

22 *Only to despite … anything.* I will try anything just to do them harm.

23 *meet* suitable

24–5 *intend a kind of zeal* put on a great show of concern

25–6 *as in love … this match* as if concerned to safeguard the honour of your brother who arranged the marriage

27 *cozened* cheated.
semblance appearance (i.e. not the reality).
maid innocent virgin

29 *instances* specific examples.
bear no less likelihood be as convincing as

30 *term me* refer to me as. This is often changed to *term me Borachio*.

33 *seeming* apparent

34 *disloyalty* unfaithfulness. *jealousy shall be called assurance* a suspicious mind will turn appearances into certainty.
preparation wedding arrangements

36 *Grow this … it can* No matter how harmful the outcome

37 *cunning* clever. *ducats* silver coins

38 *constant in the accusation* consistent in your allegation

38–9 *shame me* let me down

40 *presently* immediately

‖ • *What is Don John's mood when the scene opens: resigned, bitter, angry, irritable?*
‖ • *At what point does his attitude seem to change – and in what way?*

Don John's displeasure at the failure of his first attempt to thwart the marriage of Claudio and Hero gives way to malicious anticipation. Borachio will be seen the night before the wedding at Hero's bedroom window, thus deceiving the watching Claudio and Don Pedro into believing that Hero is dishonourable.

2:3

Benedick reflects on the folly of confirmed bachelors like Claudio who become unrecognisable when they fall in love. The conspirators begin their deception of Benedick by speaking of Beatrice's fine qualities and of her pining for his love.

5 *I am here already* i.e. no sooner said than done

‖ *Some directors have prepared the audience for the gulling of Benedick by introducing comic business with the boy.*
‖ • *What is Benedick doing during these opening lines?*
‖ • *Is the boy being cheeky in line 5 – or is Benedick teasing him in line 6?*
‖ • *We know when the boy exits (at line 6). When does he return?*

DON JOHN	What life is in that, to be the death of this marriage?	

BORACHIO The poison of that lies in you to temper. Go you to the Prince your   **15**
brother; spare not to tell him that he hath wronged his honour in
marrying the renowned Claudio – whose estimation do you mightily
hold up – to a contaminated stale, such a one as Hero.

DON JOHN What proof shall I make of that?

BORACHIO Proof enough to misuse the Prince, to vex Claudio, to undo Hero   **20**
and kill Leonato – look you for any other issue?

DON JOHN Only to despite them I will endeavour anything.

BORACHIO Go, then; find me a meet hour to draw Don Pedro and the Count
Claudio alone. Tell them that you know that Hero loves me; intend a
kind of zeal both to the Prince and Claudio – as in love of your brother's   **25**
honour who hath made this match, and his friend's reputation, who is
thus like to be cozened with the semblance of a maid – that you have
discovered thus. They will scarcely believe this without trial. Offer them
instances, which shall bear no less likelihood than to see me at her
chamber window, hear me call Margaret Hero, hear Margaret term me   **30**
Claudio. And bring them to see this the very night before the intended
wedding – for in the meantime, I will so fashion the matter that Hero
shall be absent, and there shall appear such seeming truth of Hero's
disloyalty that jealousy shall be called assurance, and all the preparation
overthrown.   **35**

DON JOHN Grow this to what adverse issue it can, I will put it in practice. Be
cunning in the working this, and thy fee is a thousand ducats.

BORACHIO Be you constant in the accusation, and my cunning shall not shame
me.

DON JOHN I will presently go learn their day of marriage.   **40**

[Exeunt

2:3   *Enter* **BENEDICK**

BENEDICK Boy!

Enter **BOY**

BOY Signor?

BENEDICK In my chamber window lies a book – bring it hither to me in the
orchard.

BOY I am here already, sir.   **5**

BENEDICK I know that, but I would have thee hence and here again.

[Exit **BOY**

I do much wonder that one man, seeing how much another man is a
fool when he dedicates his behaviours to love, will, after he hath

9	*shallow follies* silly foolishness
9–10	*become the argument of his own scorn* become the subject of his own former ridicule
11	*fife* a small flute, used with the *drum* in military marching music
12	*tabor* small drum, used with the *pipe* for dancing
14	*carving the fashion* designing the style *doublet* men's close-fitting body garment with sleeves that could be attached separately. A young man might hope to impress his lady with a fancy doublet. *was wont to* used to
15	*to the purpose* straightforwardly
16	*turned orthography* speaks in an elaborate, affected style *fantastical banquet* ornate and fanciful feast
17	*converted* transformed
18	*I will not be sworn but love may* I won't swear that love will never
19	*transform me to an oyster* shut me up in moody silence like a clam
19–20	*made an oyster* i.e. it will never happen. However, there are bawdy overtones. Oysters have long been regarded as an aphrodisiac and have also been used to allude to the female genitals.
20	*fair* beautiful
21	*I am well* i.e. unaffected by love
22	*graces* blessings
23	*grace* favour
24	*never cheapen her* not make an offer for her; not reduce her 'value' (by taking her virginity)
25	*noble, or not I for an angel* The *noble* and *angel* were Elizabethan coins. The *angel* was worth more (about half a sovereign). She must be of noble birth or Benedick wouldn't take her for a cash payment even if she were an angel. *discourse* conversation
27	*Monsieur Love* i.e. a mocking name for Claudio *arbour* trees or shrubs trained on a framework or trellis-work
30	*As hushed … grace harmony!* As if it were deliberately quiet to be in keeping with the romantic music
33	*We'll fit … pennyworth* i.e. Benedick will get more than he bargains for (probably alludes to a children's hiding and chasing game)
35	*tax not* do not strain or put a burden on
36	*slander* disgrace
37–8	*the witness still of excellency … his own perfection* the denial of a person's own accomplishments is always the proof of their high quality
39	*woo* persuade
41–3	*Since many a wooer … swear he loves* i.e. the lover will swear love to a woman whom he doesn't really value in the hope of being granted sexual favours
43	*Yet* still. *Nay, pray thee come* i.e. start your song
44	*hold longer argument* carry on the discussion

laughed at such shallow follies in others, become the argument of his
own scorn by falling in love; and such a man is Claudio. I have known 10
when there was no music with him but the drum and the fife, and now
had he rather hear the tabor and the pipe. I have known when he would
have walked ten mile afoot to see a good armour; and now will he lie
ten nights awake carving the fashion of a new doublet. He was wont to
speak plain and to the purpose (like an honest man and a soldier) and 15
now is he turned orthography; his words are a very fantastical banquet,
just so many strange dishes. May I be so converted and see with these
eyes? I cannot tell; I think not. I will not be sworn but love may
transform me to an oyster; but I'll take my oath on it, till he have made
an oyster of me, he shall never make me such a fool. One woman is fair, 20
yet I am well; another is wise, yet I am well; another virtuous, yet I am
well. But till all graces be in one woman, one woman shall not come in
my grace. Rich she shall be, that's certain; wise, or I'll none; virtuous,
or I'll never cheapen her; fair, or I'll never look on her; mild, or come
not near me; noble, or not I for an angel; of good discourse, an excellent 25
musician – and her hair shall be of what colour it please God. Ha, the
Prince of Monsieur Love! I will hide me in the arbour.

                                                                    [*He hides*

Enter DON PEDRO, LEONATO *and* CLAUDIO

DON PEDRO Come, shall we hear this music?

CLAUDIO   Yea, my good lord. How still the evening is,
        As hushed on purpose to grace harmony!   30

DON PEDRO [*Aside*] See you where Benedick hath hid himself?

CLAUDIO [*Aside*] O, very well, my lord. The music ended,
        We'll fit the hid-fox with a pennyworth.

Enter BALTHASAR, *with music*

DON PEDRO [*Aloud*] Come, Balthasar, we'll hear that song again.

BALTHASAR   O good my lord, tax not so bad a voice   35
        To slander music any more than once.

DON PEDRO It is the witness still of excellency
        To put a strange face on his own perfection.
        I pray thee sing, and let me woo no more.

BALTHASAR   Because you talk of wooing, I will sing,   40
        Since many a wooer doth commence his suit
        To her he thinks not worthy; yet he woos,
        Yet will he swear he loves.

DON PEDRO   Nay, pray thee come.
        Or if thou wilt hold longer argument,
        Do it in notes.

BALTHASAR   Note this before my notes,   45

46 *worth the noting* worth listening to

47 *crotchets* whimsical fancies (with a pun on the musical note)

48 *Note … noting* Don Pedro exclaims on the frivolity of Balthasar's worthless (*nothing*) punning.
forsooth truly

49 *divine air* heavenly tune
ravished enraptured

50 *sheep's guts* the strings for musical instruments were made from the lining of sheep's intestines
hale drag

50–1 *a horn for my money* i.e. Benedick would rather listen to a hunting horn, preferring manly soldierly stories to sentimental ones; or, at the end of the day (*when all's done*) it all leads to the cuckold's horns

57 *blithe and bonny* cheerful and carefree

59 *hey nonny, nonny* The song's refrain recommends a carefree unconcern

60 *ditties* light-hearted songs

61 *dumps* sad songs

70 *for a shift* as a makeshift when there isn't anyone better; for an improvised performance

71 *An* if

72 *bode no mischief* isn't a bad omen

73 *as lief* as soon
night-raven The raven was considered a bird that foretold disaster; a night cry would be even more ominous.

76–7 *for tomorrow night … chamber window* It was traditional to serenade newly-married couples with music on their wedding night. Here it reminds the audience that the week Leonato has said was necessary to make wedding preparations (*just seven-night* [Act 2 Scene 1 line 266]) is passing.

Many productions have introduced comic business to show Benedick's astonishment at first learning that Beatrice is in love with him (lines 80–1). The audience only can see him as he hears and responds.

- *In one film version Benedick's deckchair collapses under him.*
- *In one stage production Benedick nearly fell out of the tree where he had been drinking a bottle of wine.*

Can you think of other examples of stage business to show the effect on Benedick of what he hears?

82 *stalk on* The *fowl* or game bird being hunted is, of course, Benedick. The others are closing in stealthily for the 'kill'.

There's not a note of mine that's worth the noting.

DON PEDRO Why, these are very crotchets that he speaks;
Note notes, forsooth, and nothing.

Music

BENEDICK [*Aside*] Now, divine air! Now is his soul ravished! Is it not strange that
sheep's guts should hale souls out of men's bodies? Well, a horn for my   50
money, when all's done.

BALTHASAR *sings*

Sigh no more, ladies, sigh no more,
    Men were deceivers ever;
One foot in sea, and one on shore,
    To one thing constant never.   55
Then sigh not so, but let them go
    And be you blithe and bonny,
Converting all your sounds of woe
    Into hey nonny, nonny,

Sing no more ditties, sing no moe   60
    Of dumps so dull and heavy,
The fraud of men was ever so
    Since Summer first was leavy.
Then sigh not so, but let them go
    And be you blithe and bonny,   65
Converting all your sounds of woe
    Into hey nonny, nonny.

DON PEDRO By my troth, a good song.

BALTHASAR   And an ill singer, my lord.

DON PEDRO Ha, no, no; faith, thou sing'st well enough for a shift.   70

BENEDICK [*Aside*] An he had been a dog that should have howled thus, they
would have hanged him; and I pray God his bad voice bode no mischief.
I had as lief have heard the night-raven, come what plague could have
come after it.

DON PEDRO Yea, marry, dost thou hear, Balthasar? I pray thee, get us some   75
excellent music, for tomorrow night we would have it at the Lady
Hero's chamber window.

BALTHASAR   The best I can, my lord.

DON PEDRO Do so; farewell.

[Exit BALTHASAR

Come hither, Leonato. What was it you told me of today, that your   80
niece, Beatrice, was in love with Signor Benedick?

CLAUDIO [*Aside*] O ay, stalk on, stalk on, the fowl sits. [*Aloud*] I did never think
that lady would have loved any man.

Benedick 'noting'!

84 *dote* adore to excess

85 *in all outward behaviours* to all appearances

86 *abhor* detest

87 *Sits the wind ... corner* Is that the direction the wind blows, i.e. is that how things really are?

89 *enraged* passionate
past the infinite of thought unthinkable

90 *counterfeit* pretend

93 *the life of passion* the reality
discovers reveals

95 *Bait the hook* Benedick is now a fish to be tempted with an enticing bait.

100 *invincible* unconquerable

102 *gull* trick
but that except for the fact that
the white-bearded fellow i.e. Leonato

103 *Knavery ... reverence* surely dishonesty couldn't conceal itself in such a respectable man (age itself bestowed respect).

104 *infection* The *bait* to trap Benedick has now become a disease; he will 'catch' love.
hold it up keep it up

106 *that's her torment* that's why she's in such agony

108 *encountered him with scorn* ridiculed him when we met

110 *smock* a plain linen undergarment also worn as a nightdress

111 *writ* written

112 *pretty jest* witty joke

114–15 *she found ... between the sheet* Leonato puns on a *sheet* of paper and bed-sheet.

116 *That* That's the one

117 *halfpence* tiny pieces (a *halfpence* was a small silver coin)
railed at scolded

118 *immodest* lacking in self-respect

119 *flout* scorn
measure judge

123 *ecstasy* frenzy

124 *overborne* overwhelmed
afeard afraid

124–5 *a desperate outrage* frantic violence

LEONATO	No, nor I neither, but most wonderful that she should so dote on Signor Benedick, whom she hath, in all outward behaviours, seemed ever to abhor.	85

BENEDICK [*Aside*] Is't possible? Sits the wind in that corner.

LEONATO By my troth, my lord, I cannot tell what to think of it, but that she loves him with an enraged affection – it is past the infinite of thought.

DON PEDRO Maybe she doth but counterfeit? 90

CLAUDIO Faith, like enough.

LEONATO O God, counterfeit? There was never counterfeit of passion came so near the life of passion as she discovers it.

DON PEDRO Why, what effects of passion shows she?

CLAUDIO [*Aside*] Bait the hook well, this fish will bite. 95

LEONATO What effects, my lord? She will sit you – you heard my daughter tell you how.

CLAUDIO She did indeed.

DON PEDRO How, how, I pray you? You amaze me; I would have thought her spirit had been invincible against all assaults of affection. 100

LEONATO I would have sworn it had, my lord, especially against Benedick.

BENEDICK [*Aside*] I should think this a gull but that the white-bearded fellow speaks it. Knavery cannot, sure, hide himself in such reverence.

CLAUDIO [*Aside*] He hath ta'en the infection; hold it up.

DON PEDRO Hath she made her affection known to Benedick? 105

LEONATO No, and swears she never will – that's her torment.

CLAUDIO 'Tis true indeed, so your daughter says. 'Shall I,' says she, 'that have so oft encountered him with scorn, write to him that I love him?'

LEONATO This says she now, when she is beginning to write to him, for she'll be up twenty times a night, and there will she sit in her smock, till she have writ a sheet of paper. My daughter tells us all. 110

CLAUDIO Now you talk of a sheet of paper, I remember a pretty jest your daughter told us of.

LEONATO O when she had writ it and was reading it over, she found 'Benedick' and 'Beatrice' between the sheet? 115

CLAUDIO That.

LEONATO O, she tore the letter into a thousand halfpence, railed at herself, that she should be so immodest to write to one that she knew would flout her. 'I measure him,' says she, 'by my own spirit; for I should flout him if he writ to me – yea, though I love him, I should.' 120

CLAUDIO Then down upon her knees she falls, weeps, sobs, beats her heart, tears her hair, prays, curses, 'O sweet Benedick – God give me patience!'

LEONATO She doth indeed, my daughter says so; and the ecstasy hath so much overborne her that my daughter is sometime afeard she will do a desperate outrage to herself. It is very true. 125

126	*were good* would be a good thing.
	knew of it by some other heard about it from someone else
127	*discover* tell
128	*make but a sport of it* only make a joke about it
130	*An* if
	an alms a good deed
131	*out of all suspicion* without any doubt
134	*blood* passion
	combating fighting
137	*bestowed this dotage* given her affection
137–8	*daffed all other respects … myself* set aside all other considerations (such as Beatrice's social inferiority to himself) and married her myself
139	*'a* he

In Act 2 Scene 1 (line 244) Don Pedro had proposed marriage to Beatrice. Here he again says that he wishes Beatrice was in love with him. How serious is he? Are the circumstances of the present situation different from the earlier occasion?

140	*Were it good, think you?* Do you think that's a good idea?
142	*ere* before
143–4	*rather than … crossness* rather than give up any of her usual scorn
145	*She doth well* She's right
	make tender of offer
147	*contemptible spirit* disdainful nature
148	*proper* fine
149	*He hath indeed a good outward happiness* He is certainly outwardly good-looking.
150	*Before God* an exclamation expressing strong agreement
	in my mind in my opinion
151	*sparks* glimmers
153	*Hector* the Trojan warrior hero
154	*with great discretion* with considerable prudence (i.e. he avoids those he is likely to lose)
155	*Christian-like fear* Christians were instructed to avoid violence (though Don Pedro rashly suggests that Benedick's Christian principles are a convenient justification for his cowardice)
158	*And so will he do* that's the way he does
159	*large jests* crude jokes
161	*let her wear … counsel* let her suffer and overcome it with sensible reflection
163	*by* from
164	*modestly* humbly

DON PEDRO It were good that Benedick knew of it by some other, if she will not discover it.

CLAUDIO   To what end? He would make but a sport of it and torment the poor lady worse.

DON PEDRO An he should, it were an alms to hang him. She's an excellent sweet 130
lady and, out of all suspicion, she is virtuous.

CLAUDIO   And she is exceeding wise.

DON PEDRO In everything but in loving Benedick.

LEONATO   O my lord, wisdom and blood combating in so tender a body, we
have ten proofs to one that blood hath the victory. I am sorry for her, as 135
I have just cause, being her uncle and her guardian.

DON PEDRO I would she had bestowed this dotage on me; I would have daffed
all other respects and made her half myself. I pray you tell Benedick of
it, and hear what 'a will say.

LEONATO   Were it good, think you? 140

CLAUDIO   Hero thinks surely she will die; for she says she will die if he love
her not; and she will die ere she make her love known; and she will die
if he woo her – rather than she will bate one breath of her accustomed
crossness.

DON PEDRO She doth well. If she should make tender of her love, 'tis very 145
possible he'll scorn it, for the man – as you know all – hath a
contemptible spirit.

CLAUDIO   He is a very proper man.

DON PEDRO He hath indeed a good outward happiness.

CLAUDIO   Before God, and in my mind, very wise. 150

DON PEDRO He doth indeed show some sparks that are like wit.

CLAUDIO   And I take him to be valiant.

DON PEDRO As Hector, I assure you; and in the managing of quarrels you may
say he is wise, for either he avoids them with great discretion, or
undertakes them with a most Christian-like fear. 155

LEONATO   If he do fear God, 'a must necessarily keep peace. If he break the
peace, he ought to enter into a quarrel with fear and trembling.

DON PEDRO And so will he do, for the man doth fear God, howsoever it seems
not in him by some large jests he will make. Well, I am sorry for your
niece; shall we go seek Benedick, and tell him of her love? 160

CLAUDIO   Never tell him, my lord; let her wear it out with good counsel.

LEONATO   Nay, that's impossible; she may wear her heart out first.

DON PEDRO Well, we will hear further of it by your daughter. Let it cool the
while, I love Benedick well, and I could wish he would modestly
examine himself, to see how much he is unworthy so good a lady. 165

LEONATO   My lord, will you walk? Dinner is ready.

Much Ado About Nothing

167 *upon this* as the result of this
never trust my expectation never believe
that I can make predictions about anything

168 *net* used to trap birds

169 *carry* carry out

169–70 *when they hold … dotage* when each
believes the other to be madly in love

170 *and no such matter* when there's no such
thing

171 *would see* would like to see.
merely a dumb show just like a mime

173 *the conference was sadly borne* the
conversation was carried out seriously

> How should the sentence **This can be no trick** (line 173) be delivered: hesitantly, smugly, suspiciously, in horrified surprise?

175 *have their full bent* are stretched to the limit

176 *requited* repaid, returned. *censured*
judged. *bear myself proudly* behave
scornfully

179 *their detractions* criticisms of themselves

181 *reprove* deny. *but for* except for

> Make a note of Beatrice's virtues that Benedick lists in lines 180–2 then compare them with the qualities he said he would require in his ideal woman (lines 20–26). What conclusions do you draw?

183 *argument* proof

184 *chance* possibly. *odd quirks* irrelevant
jibes. *remnants of wit* feeble witticisms

185 *railed … against* criticised

186–7 *in his age* as a mature man

187 *quips and sentences* jokes and proverbial
clichés. *paper bullets* i.e. harmless

187–8 *awe a man … humour* frighten a man
from what he really wants

191 *marks* signs

> At this point Benedick is convinced that Beatrice is in love with him; Beatrice, of course, knows nothing of his changed feelings.
>
> How might Benedick behave here? Would he try to impress Beatrice? How? How might Beatrice react to the new Benedick? Would she be suspicious? Read the parts aloud to convey their different perspectives. Can you think of suitable business to reinforce their respective attitudes?

198 *daw* jackdaw.
stomach appetite – for dinner or for
another verbal sparring match?

203 *Jew* In Shakespeare's day Jews were
unpopular and often persecuted.
picture portrait

> Compare this scene with the tricking of Hero in the next scene (Act 3 Scene 1).

> • The second scene is wholly in blank verse whereas the tricking of Benedick is in prose. Why, do you think?
> • Can you find other differences in emphasis and/or style?

*Don Pedro's plan is put into effect. Benedick hides and hears Beatrice's virtues praised and his own scorn condemned. Benedick is astonished but resolves to be **horribly in love with her** (line 183) and desperately looks for signs of love in her when she comes to summon him to dinner.*

They move out of **BENEDICK'S** *hearing*

CLAUDIO   If he do not dote on her upon this, I will never trust my expectation.

DON PEDRO Let there be the same net spread for her, and that must your
daughter and her gentlewomen carry. The sport will be when they hold
one an opinion of another's dotage, and no such matter; that's the scene   170
that I would see, which will be merely a dumb show. Let us send her to
call him in to dinner.

[*Exeunt* **DON PEDRO**, **CLAUDIO**, *and* **LEONATO**

BENEDICK [*Coming forward*] This can be no trick. The conference was sadly borne.
They have the truth of this from Hero. They seem to pity the lady; it
seems her affections have their full bent. Love me? Why, it must be   175
requited! I hear how I am censured; they say I will bear myself proudly
if I perceive the love come from her. They say, too, that she will rather
die than give any sign of affection. I did never think to marry. I must not
seem proud. Happy are they that hear their detractions and can put
them to mending! They say the lady is fair – 'tis a truth, I can bear them   180
witness. And virtuous – 'tis so, I cannot reprove it. And wise – but for
loving me. By my troth, it is no addition to her wit; nor no great
argument of her folly, for I will be horribly in love with her. I may
chance have some odd quirks and remnants of wit broken on me
because I have railed so long against marriage. But doth not the appetite   185
alter? A man loves the meat in his youth that he cannot endure in his
age. Shall quips and sentences, and these paper bullets of the brain, awe
a man from the career of his humour? No – the world must be peopled.
When I said I would die a bachelor, I did not think I should live till I
were married. Here comes Beatrice.   190

Enter **BEATRICE**

By this day, she's a fair lady! I do spy some marks of love in her.

BEATRICE   Against my will I am sent to bid you come in to dinner.

BENEDICK   Fair Beatrice, I thank you for your pains.

BEATRICE   I took no more pains for those thanks than you take pains to thank
me; if it had been painful I would not have come.   195

BENEDICK   You take pleasure, then, in the message?

BEATRICE   Yea, just so much as you may take upon a knife's point, and choke a
daw withal. You have no stomach, signor? Fare you well.

[*Exit*

BENEDICK   Ha! 'Against my will I am sent to bid you come in to dinner' –
there's a double meaning in that. 'I took no more pains for those thanks   200
than you took pains to thank me' – that's as much as to say, 'Any pains
that I take for you is as easy as thanks.' If I do not take pity of her, I am
a villain. If I do not love her, I am a Jew. I will go get her picture.

[*Exit*

3:1

Don Pedro's plan continues. Beatrice is lured to the orchard and overhears Hero and Ursula discussing Benedick's love for her and his fear of Beatrice's scornful nature. Beatrice is amazed and resolves to return Benedick's love.

1 *parlour* a small family room adjoining the large hall

3 *Proposing with* in conversation with

4 *Ursley* an informal version of Ursula

5 *discourse* conversation

7 *steal* creep
pleachèd bower i.e. the same arbour of intertwining branches used by Benedick (see Act 2 Scene 3 line 27)

9–11 *like favourites … bred it* a common political metaphor alluding to the way in which a ruler might win the support of courtiers by granting favours but then become dependent on and therefore lose control of them

12 *propose* conversation
office job, responsibility

13 *Bear thee well in it* carry it out properly

14 *warrant* assure.
presently immediately

16 *trace this alley up and down* stroll backwards and forwards along this path

19 *merit* deserve

21 *matter* substance, material

23 *hearsay* rumour

24 *lapwing* a bird that runs in a scurrying manner when on the ground

26 *angling* fishing

27 *oars* fins

30 *couchèd … coverture* hidden in the cover made by the honeysuckle

31 *Fear you not … dialogue* Don't worry, I'll play my part in the conversation

34 *disdainful* mocking, scornful

35 *coy* shy, reserved

36 *haggards of the rock* wild female hawks

3:1   *Enter* **HERO**, **MARGARET** *and* **URSULA**

HERO   Good Margaret, run thee to the parlour;
                There shalt thou find my cousin Beatrice
                Proposing with the Prince and Claudio.
                Whisper her ear and tell her I and Ursley
                Walk in the orchard, and our whole discourse   5
                Is all of her. Say that thou overheardst us
                And bid her steal into the pleachèd bower,
                Where honeysuckles, ripened by the sun,
                Forbid the sun to enter – like favourites
                Made proud by princes, that advance their pride   10
                Against that power that bred it. There will she hide her
                To listen our propose. This is thy office;
                Bear thee well in it, and leave us alone.

MARGARET   I'll make her come, I warrant you, presently.

                                                        [*Exit*

HERO   Now, Ursula, when Beatrice doth come,   15
                As we do trace this alley up and down,
                Our talk must only by of Benedick.
                When I do name him, let it be thy part
                To praise him more than ever man did merit.
                My talk to thee must be how Benedick   20
                Is sick in love with Beatrice. Of this matter
                Is little Cupid's crafty arrow made,
                That only wounds by hearsay –

                        Enter **BEATRICE**, *behind*

                                Now begin;
                For look where Beatrice like a lapwing runs
                Close by the ground, to hear our conference.   25

URSULA [*Aside to* **HERO**] The pleasant'st angling is to see the fish
                Cut with her golden oars the silver stream,
                And greedily devour the treacherous bait;
                So angle we for Beatrice, who even now
                Is couchèd in the woodbine coverture.   30
                Fear you not my part of the dialogue.

HERO   [*Aside*] Then go we near her, that her ear lose nothing
                Of the false sweet bait that we lay for it.

                        They approach the bower

                [*Aloud*] No truly, Ursula, she is too disdainful;
                I know her spirits are as coy and wild   35
                As haggards of the rock.

URSULA   But are you sure
                That Benedick loves Beatrice so entirely?

38 *new-trothèd* newly betrothed (i.e. Claudio)

42 *To wish him wrestle with affection* to urge him to struggle with his love (i.e. for Beatrice) and overcome it

44–6 *Doth not … couch upon?* i.e. Doesn't Benedick deserve a wife at least as good as Beatrice? (*bed* = marriage-bed)

48 *As much as may be yielded to a man* A deliberately ambiguous line which plays cunningly on different meanings of *may* and *yielded*: *can* be yielded (i.e. given sexually); *should* be given (i.e. morally); as much as it is *wise* to give (sceptical).

52 *Misprising* despising. *wit* cleverness

54 *All matter else seems weak* everything else seems inferior to herself

55 *Nor take … affection* she cannot consider the form nor even the idea of love

56 *self-endeared* in love with herself

How might Beatrice react to this speech (lines 47–56): hurt, surprised, shocked, angry, offended, dismissive, disbelieving?

- *The text gives no words to Beatrice during the tricking episode. How would you convey her feelings by gestures and facial expression? One Beatrice clawed at her critics and beat her head against the orchard wall.*
- *Another Beatrice let out an involuntary 'Oh!'. What tone would you have used?*

---

60 *how rarely featured* however good-looking

61 *spell him backward* turn his good points back to front. It was believed that witches could raise the devil by saying prayers backwards.

62 *should be her sister* was her sister (i.e. effeminate)

63 *black* dark-skinned

63–4 *drawing of an antic … blot* while trying to design some bizarre figure created only an ugly blob

64 *a lance ill-headed* a spear with a badly-made point

65 *low* short
agate very vilely cut a badly-carved agate stone (an allusion to the small figures cut in agates used for seals)

66 *vane* weather-cock
blown with all winds implies that the speaker holds superficial and wavering views

67 *block movèd with none* a senseless lump incapable of mental activity

69–70 *never gives … purchaseth* i.e. she never gives credit its due recognition

70 *simpleness* honesty

71 *carping* fault-finding. *commendable* praiseworthy

72 *odd* eccentric. *from all fashions* out of step with all conventions

75 *mock me into air* annihilate me with her ridicule

76 *Out of myself* i.e. silence me
press me to death An accused person who refused to answer the charge might have heavy weights loaded onto him to persuade him to talk.

77–8 *covered fire … inwardly* a covered fire would smoulder unseen rather than burn in flames. Hero says Benedick will have to smother his passion which will gradually burn him up and destroy from within.

79 *die with mocks* be killed by ridicule

HERO	So says the Prince, and my new-trothèd lord.	
URSULA	And did they bid you tell her of it, madam?	
HERO	They did entreat me to acquaint her of it;	40
	But I persuaded them, if they loved Benedick,	
	To wish him wrestle with affection	
	And never to let Beatrice know of it.	
URSULA	Why did you so? Doth not the gentleman	
	Deserve as full as fortunate a bed	45
	As ever Beatrice shall couch upon?	
HERO	O god of love! I know he doth deserve	
	As much as may be yielded to a man.	
	But Nature never framed a woman's heart	
	Of prouder stuff than that of Beatrice.	50
	Disdain and scorn ride sparkling in her eyes,	
	Misprising what they look on; and her wit	
	Values itself so highly, that to her	
	All matter else seems weak. She cannot love,	
	Nor take no shape nor project of affection,	55
	She is so self-endeared.	
URSULA	Sure I think so;	
	And therefore certainly it were not good	
	She knew his love, lest she'll make sport at it.	
HERO	Why, you speak truth. I never yet saw man,	
	How wise, how noble, young, how rarely featured,	60
	But she would spell him backward. If fair-faced,	
	She would swear the gentleman should be her sister;	
	If black, why Nature, drawing of an antic,	
	Made a foul blot; if tall, a lance ill-headed;	
	If low, an agate very vilely cut;	65
	If speaking, why, a vane blown with all winds;	
	If silent, why, a block movèd with none;	
	So turns she every man the wrong side out,	
	And never gives to truth and virtue that	
	Which simpleness and merit purchaseth.	70
URSULA	Sure, sure, such carping is not commendable.	
HERO	No, not to be so odd and from all fashions	
	As Beatrice is, cannot be commendable.	
	But who dare tell her so? If I should speak	
	She would mock me into air; O, she would laugh me	75
	Out of myself, press me to death with wit.	
	Therefore let Benedick, like covered fire,	
	Consume away in sighs, waste inwardly.	
	It were a better death than die with mocks,	
	Which is as bad as die with tickling.	80

84 *devise some honest slanders* invent some minor slurs against Beatrice (i.e. not ones that would dishonour her)

Here Hero speaks of making up some **honest slanders** to reduce the love-struck Benedick's opinion of Beatrice. Compare this with the serious slanders planned against Hero herself. It is a dreadful irony.

85–6 *One doth not know ... liking* It's amazing how much love can be damaged by such criticism

90 *prized to have* valued for having

92 *the only man in Italy* the 'main man'

95 *Speaking my fancy* speaking my mind

96 *argument* sharpness of reasoning

99 *excellence* distinction. *earn* deserve. *ere* before

101 *every day tomorrow* after tomorrow, every day

102 *attires* head-dresses. *counsel* advice

103 *furnish* trim

104 *limed* caught. Spreading sticky bird-lime on the branches of trees was a common way of trapping birds.

105 *haps* chance

107 *What fire is in mine ears* Beatrice's ears are 'burning' with embarrassment because she has been talked about so scathingly; also, possibly, the *fire* of newly-kindled passion.

109 *Contempt, farewell!* Beatrice instantly renounces her habitual scornful manner.

110 *No glory ... back of such.* Nothing creditable is ever said behind the back of those who are proud and scornful.

111 *requite* return (i.e. Benedick's love)

112 *Taming my wild heart ... hand* Hero had compared Beatrice to a *haggard* or wild hawk (line 36); now Beatrice uses the same metaphor to indicate that she will abandon her wildness and submit to Benedick's love.

113 *incite* encourage

114 *bind our loves up* join our two loves together. *holy band* wedding ring (i.e. marriage)

116 *better than reportingly* more than I have heard others describe (i.e. she herself knows it to be true)

This last speech marks a turning point in Beatrice's life. Her use of verse for the first time points to its importance. How should it be delivered?

Some Beatrices have had to deliver it soaking wet from a garden pool or hose or dishevelled from hiding in hedges. Would you introduce a comic flavour?
* Is she reflective, excited, serious, restrained, stunned, elated?
* How would Beatrice exit: solemnly, skipping with excitement, briskly as if she's made up her mind?

Don Pedro's trick has worked and Beatrice and Benedick have each declared that they will return the other's love. We might expect a conventionally romantic scene the next time they meet. Compare this with the actual circumstances of their next meeting (Act 4 Scene 1 lines 250-312).

Beatrice is tricked into the orchard where she hears Benedick's virtues praised and her own scornful nature condemned. Hero claims that Benedick should be discouraged from declaring his love for Beatrice lest he be mercilessly mocked. Beatrice is shocked and determines to reform and return Benedick's love.

URSULA	Yet tell her of it; hear what she will say.
HERO	No; rather I will go to Benedick
	And counsel him to fight against his passion.
	And truly, I'll devise some honest slanders
	To stain my cousin with. One doth not know 85
	How much an ill word may empoison liking.
URSULA	O, do not do your cousin such a wrong!
	She cannot be so much without true judgement –
	Having so swift and excellent a wit
	As she is prized to have – as to refuse 90
	So rare a gentleman as Signor Benedick.
HERO	He is the only man in Italy,
	Always excepted my dear Claudio.
URSULA	I pray you be not angry with me, madam,
	Speaking my fancy: Signor Benedick 95
	For shape, for bearing, argument and valour,
	Goes foremost in report through Italy.
HERO	Indeed he hath an excellent good name.
URSULA	His excellence did earn it, ere he had it.
	When are you married, madam? 100
HERO	Why, every day tomorrow. Come, go in.
	I'll show thee some attires, and have thy counsel
	Which is the best to furnish me tomorrow.

They move out of BEATRICE'S *hearing*

URSULA	She's limed, I warrant you; we have caught her, madam!
HERO	If it prove so, then loving goes by haps. 105
	Some Cupid kills with arrows, some with traps.

[Exeunt HERO *and* URSULA

BEATRICE *[Coming forward]* What fire is in mine ears? Can this be true?
Stand I condemned for pride and scorn so much?
Contempt, farewell! And maiden pride, adieu!
  No glory lives behind the back of such. 110
And, Benedick, love on; I will requite thee,
  Taming my wild heart to thy loving hand.
If thou dost love, my kindness shall incite thee
  To bind our loves up in a holy band;
For others say thou dost deserve, and I 115
Believe it better than reportingly.

[Exit

3:2

Don Pedro and Claudio feign amazement at Benedick's transformation to the conventional 'lover' and tease him mercilessly. As Benedick leaves with Leonato to raise the subject of marriage, Don John reveals his news of Hero's supposed unfaithfulness.

1	*consummate* completed
3	*bring* accompany. *vouchsafe* allow
4	*as great a soil in the new gloss* tarnish the freshness as much
5–6	*only be bold* trouble only
7–8	*cut Cupid's bowstring* i.e. and so avoided falling in love
8	*hangman* rogue
9	*clapper* the 'tongue' of a bell which makes the sound as it strikes it on the inside
11	*Gallants* gentlemen
13	*hope* think
14	*truant* deserter. *blood* passion
15	*wants* lacks, i.e. he's hard up
17	*Draw it.* Pull it out.
18	*Hang it!* i.e. the tooth would have to be tied with thread before it could be drawn
19	*You must … afterwards* Claudio puns on the gruesome and barbaric practice of hanging, drawing (i.e. disembowelling) and quartering of those convicted of treason.
21	*a humour or a worm* both were thought to cause tooth decay
22	*master a grief* overcome a pain

> Compare the circumstances of Benedick's line **everyone can master a grief** *but he that has it* (line 22) with those in which Leonato expresses similar sentiments in Act 5 Scene 1 (lines 35–6). Notice the curious shared reference to the 'toothache'.

24	*fancy* love; whim. *a fancy* inclination
25	*strange disguises* i.e. Benedick has taken a sudden interest in clothes. Don Pedro anticipates his mimicking foreign fashions.
27	*all slops* large loose breeches
29	*no fool for fancy* not under the command of love
30–1	*old signs* familiar symptoms
31	*A* he. *'a* in the. *bode* mean

- *How would you stage the taunting of Benedick? Would Claudio and Don Pedro speak with open/suppressed laughter, mock-seriousness, apparent disbelief?*
- *Look at the clues we are given about Benedick's changed appearance and manner. What pieces of comic business do they suggest to you?*
- *How does Benedick react to his friends' taunts: is he visibly embarrassed, coldly dignified, irritated, angry?*

36	*civet* perfume (from the African civet-cat)
38	*note* sign. *melancholy* (the traditional feature of the lover)

3:2   *Enter* **DON PEDRO**, **CLAUDIO**, **BENEDICK** *and* **LEONATO**

DON PEDRO I do but stay till your marriage be consummate, and then go I toward Arragon.

CLAUDIO   I'll bring you thither, my lord, if you'll vouchsafe me.

DON PEDRO Nay, that would as great a soil in the new gloss of your marriage, as to show a child his new coat and forbid him to wear it. I will only be   **5** bold with Benedick for his company; for, from the crown of his head to the sole of his foot, he is all mirth. He hath twice or thrice cut Cupid's bowstring, and the little hangman dare not shoot at him; he hath a heart as sound as a bell and his tongue is the clapper – for what his heart thinks, his tongue speaks.   **10**

BENEDICK   Gallants, I am not as I have been.

LEONATO   So say I – methinks you are sadder.

CLAUDIO   I hope he be in love.

DON PEDRO Hang him, truant! There's no true drop of blood in him to be truly touched with love. If he be sad, he wants money.   **15**

BENEDICK   I have the toothache.

DON PEDRO Draw it.

BENEDICK   Hang it!

CLAUDIO   You must hang it first, and draw it afterwards.

DON PEDRO What – sigh for the toothache?   **20**

LEONATO   Where is but a humour or a worm.

BENEDICK   Well, everyone can master a grief but he that has it.

CLAUDIO   Yet say I, he is in love.

DON PEDRO There is no appearance of fancy in him, unless it be a fancy that he hath to strange disguises, as to be a Dutchman today, a Frenchman   **25** tomorrow, or in the shape of two countries at once, as a German from the waist downward, all slops, and a Spaniard from the hip upward, no doublet. Unless he have a fancy to this foolery, as it appears he hath, he is no fool for fancy, as you would have it appear he is.

CLAUDIO   If he be not in love with some woman, there is no believing old   **30** signs. 'A brushes his hat 'a mornings – what should that bode?

DON PEDRO Hath any man seen him at the barber's?

CLAUDIO   No, but the barber's man hath been seen with him, and the old ornament of his cheek hath already stuffed tennis balls.

LEONATO   Indeed he looks younger than he did, by the loss of a beard.   **35**

DON PEDRO Nay, 'a rubs himself with civet; can you smell him out by that?

CLAUDIO   That's as much as to say the sweet youth's in love.

DON PEDRO The greatest note of it is his melancholy.

CLAUDIO   And when was he wont to wash his face?

40 *paint himself* use make-up
    For the which on the subject of which

42 *which is now crept into a lute string* i.e. he is now more
    interested in love songs

43 *governed by stops* ruled by the frets on the lute

44 *tells a heavy tale for him* tells a sorry story of him

47 *warrant* guarantee
    one that knows him not doesn't know his real character; doesn't
    know him sexually

48 *ill conditions* bad habits
    dies wastes away; a common term for sexual orgasm

49 *buried with her face upward* having 'died' in the sexual sense on
    her back, *buried* beneath Benedick

50 *charm* cure

51 *studied* learned by heart

52 *hobby-horses* buffoons

53 *For my life* I would bet my life on it (that he intends)
    break discuss

54 *'Tis even so* that's right
    Margaret probably a mistake for Ursula
    by this by this time

55 *the two bears ... another* probably adapted from the proverb:
    'One wolf will not bite another'

*Don John's entrance marks an abrupt change of mood from the
facetious mocking of Benedick.*

- *Does the mood change as soon as he enters or do the former
  high spirits continue for a short time?*
- *How does Claudio react: with astonishment, bewilderment,
  disbelief, anger (reaching for his sword, making to hit Don
  John)?*

58 *Good den* i.e. 'God give you good evening'

59 *If your leisure served* if you have the time

67 *impediment* obstacle
    discover reveal

68 *let that appear hereafter* let the future show that

68–9 *aim better at me* judge me more accurately

69 *by that I now will manifest* by what I will now reveal

70 *holds you well* thinks highly of you
    holp helped
    effect bring about

71 *suit ill-spent ... ill-bestowed* a waste of time and effort

73 *circumstances shortened* leaving out the details

73–4 *for she has been ... a-talking of* for she has been the subject of
    discussion for too long

74 *Disloyal* unfaithful

Don Pedro	Yea, or to paint himself? For the which, I hear what they say of him.	**40**
Claudio	Nay, but his jesting spirit, which is now crept into a lute string and now governed by stops?	
Don Pedro	Indeed, that tells a heavy tale for him. Conclude, conclude – he is in love.	**45**
Claudio	Nay, but I know who loves him.	
Don Pedro	That would I know too; I warrant one that knows him not.	
Claudio	Yes, and his ill conditions, and in despite of all, dies for him.	
Don Pedro	She shall be buried with her face upwards.	
Benedick	Yet is this no charm for the toothache. Old signor, walk aside with me: I have studied eight or nine wise words to speak to you which these hobby-horses must not hear.	**50**

[Exeunt **Benedick** *and* **Leonato**

Don Pedro	For my life, to break with him about Beatrice.	
Claudio	'Tis even so; Hero and Margaret have by this played their parts with Beatrice; and then the two bears will not bite one another when they meet.	**55**

Enter **Don John**

Don John	My lord and brother, God save you!	
Don Pedro	Good den, brother.	
Don John	If your leisure served, I would speak with you.	
Don Pedro	In private?	**60**
Don John	If it please you. Yet Count Claudio may hear, for what I would speak of concerns him.	
Don Pedro	What's the matter?	
Don John	*[To* **Claudio***]* Means your lordship to be married tomorrow?	
Don Pedro	You know he does.	**65**
Don John	I know not that, when he knows what I know.	
Claudio	If there be any impediment I pray you discover it.	
Don John	You may think I love you not; let that appear hereafter, and aim better at me by that I now will manifest. For my brother – I think he holds you well and in dearness of heart – hath help to effect your ensuing marriage: surely suit ill-spent and labour ill-bestowed?	**70**
Don Pedro	Why, what's the matter?	
Don John	I came hither to tell you, and circumstances shortened – for she has been too long a-talking of – the lady is disloyal.	
Claudio	Who – Hero?	**75**
Don John	Even she. Leonato's Hero; your Hero; every man's Hero.	
Claudio	Disloyal?	

78 *paint out* show fully
79 *fit her to it* show how it applies to her
80 *warrant* proof
82 *then* still. *fit your honour* suit someone of your position
86 *that* what. *confess not that you know* admit that you don't know anything
87 *enough* i.e. to convince you
93–4 *Bear it coldly but till* endure this (knowledge) calmly only until
95 *untowardly turned* shamefully changed
96 *mischief strangely thwarting* wickedness that unnaturally ruins
98 *the sequel* the outcome, i.e. the 'evidence'

> The text does not present the **amiable encounter** between Borachio and Margaret that deceives Claudio and Don Pedro. One film version shows images of their love-making superimposed over the final speeches of the scene.
>
> How might the meeting be suggested in a stage production: projected photographs, off-stage sound, music, lighting?
> What would be the effect of representing the assignation?

Don John claims that the 'proof' of his accusations will be in what Claudio and Don Pedro see with their own eyes at Hero's bedroom window.
• Are the eyes and ears always reliable? What other examples of mistaken 'noting' have we seen already?

Benedick appears, having adopted the appearance and behaviour of the lover, and has to suffer in silence the mockery of his friends. The mood changes abruptly when Don John announces Hero's supposed faithlessness and challenges them to confirm this with the evidence of their own eyes.

3:3

Constable Dogberry assembles the Watch and instructs them with a muddled account of their duties. When they are left to mount the watch they overhear the drunken Borachio bragging to Conrade about the successful deception of Claudio and Don Pedro.

The Watch.

s.d. *the Watch* a group of local citizens chosen to keep law and order. They were not a professional body like a modern police force and were often the targets of ridicule.

2 *or else … should* if not, it's a pity for they will. *salvation* (for *damnation*)

5 *allegiance* (for *lack of allegiance* or duty)

7 *desartless* without merit (for *most deserving*). *constable* i.e. the man in charge

10 *well-favoured* good looking (for *favoured* i.e. blessed). *gift of fortune* good luck

11 *nature* intrinsic ability. The relationship between Fortune and Nature was a common debating subject. Characteristically Dogberry's 'logic' here attributes them wrongly.

DON JOHN   The word is too good to paint out her wickedness. I could say she were worse – think you of a worse title, and I will fit her to it. Wonder not till further warrant. Go but with me tonight, you shall see her   **80**
chamber window entered, even the night before her wedding day. If you love her then, tomorrow wed her; but it would better fit your honour to change your mind.

CLAUDIO   May this be so?

DON PEDRO   I will not think it.   **85**

DON JOHN   If you dare not trust that you see, confess not that you know. If you will follow me, I will show you enough; and when you have seen more and heard more, proceed accordingly.

CLAUDIO   If I see anything tonight why I should not marry her tomorrow, in the congregation where I should wed, there will I shame her.   **90**

DON PEDRO   And as I wooed for thee to obtain her, I will join with thee to disgrace her.

DON JOHN   I will disparage her no farther till you are my witnesses. Bear it coldly but till midnight, and let the issue show itself.

DON PEDRO   O day untowardly turned!   **95**

CLAUDIO   O mischief strangely thwarting!

DON JOHN   O plague right well prevented! So will you say when you have seen the sequel.

[Exeunt

3:3   *Enter* **DOGBERRY, VERGES,** *with the* **WATCH**

DOGBERRY   Are you good men and true?

VERGES   Yea, or else it were pity but they should suffer salvation, body and soul.   **5**

DOGBERRY   Nay, that were a punishment too good for them, if they should have any allegiance in them, being chosen for the Prince's watch.

VERGES   Well, give them their charge, neighbour Dogberry.

DOGBERRY   First, who think you the most desartless man to be constable?

FIRST WATCH   Hugh Oatcake, sir, or George Seacoal, for they can write and read.   **10**

DOGBERRY   Come hither, neighbour Seacoal; God hath blessed you with a good name. To be a well-favoured man is the gift of fortune, but to write and read comes by nature.

SECOND WATCH   Both which, Master Constable –

Much Ado About Nothing

> Dogberry is very pompous and self-important. How could you suggest this in the staging of this scene?
> - His costume: uniform, staff of office, medals, hat, weapon?
> - His position on stage: raised above?
> - Contrast with Verges: physical size, voice, costume?
> - The way the other Watch members react to him: are they scared of him?

13	*favour* looks
16	*senseless* (for *sensible*)
	fit suitable
17	*bear you* you carry
18	*comprehend* (for *apprehend*)
	vagrom (for *vagrant* or homeless)
	bid any man stand order anyone to halt
20	*'a* he
21	*note* notice
	presently immediately
23	*is none* isn't one
25	*True … subjects* i.e. they need not trouble themselves with criminals!
	meddle interfere
27	*tolerable* (for *intolerable*)
30	*ancient* experienced
31	*bills* the Watch's weapons, like a halberd, a spear-point combined with an axe-head mounted on a long shaft
40	*no true man* not honest
41	*the more is for your honesty* the greater is your own honesty
42	*lay hands on him* arrest him
43–4	*they that touch pitch will be defiled* The proverb 'He that toucheth pitch shall be defiled' comes from the Bible (Ecclesiastes Chapter 13 verse 1) where it means that someone who associates with immoral or corrupt people will be corrupted themselves. Pitch is a black sticky substance obtained by boiling tar. It was painted on the undersides of ships to make the seams between the wooden planks watertight. Anyone touching wet pitch would be soiled or made dirty.
44	*defiled* tainted, corrupted
45	*steal* creep
47	*by my will* by my choice
	much more (for *much less*)

DOGBERRY   You have. I knew it would be your answer. Well, for your favour, sir, why, give God thanks and make no boast of it; and for your writing and reading, let that appear when there is no need of such vanity. You are thought here to be the most senseless and fit man for the constable of the Watch; therefore, bear you the lantern. This is your charge: you shall comprehend all vagrom men; you are to bid any man stand, in the Prince's name.   **15**

SECOND WATCH How if 'a will not stand?   **20**

DOGBERRY   Why then, take no note of him, but let him go; and presently call the rest of the watch together and thank God you are rid of a knave.

VERGES   If he will not stand when he is bidden, he is none of the Prince's subjects.

DOGBERRY   True, and they are to meddle with none but the Prince's subjects.   **25**
You shall also make no noise in the streets; for, for the watch to babble and to talk is most tolerable and not to be endured.

SECOND WATCH We will rather sleep than talk; we know what belongs to a watch.

DOGBERRY   Why, you speak like an ancient and most quiet watchman, for I   **30**
cannot see how sleeping should offend; only, have a care that your bills be not stolen. Well, you are to call at all the alehouses and bid those that are drunk get them to bed.

FIRST WATCH How if they will not?

DOGBERRY   Why, then let them alone till they are sober. If they make you not   **35**
then the better answer, you may say they are not the men you took them for.

FIRST WATCH Well, sir.

DOGBERRY   If you meet a thief you may suspect him, by virtue of your office, to be no true man; and for such kind of men, the less you meddle or make   **40**
with them, why, the more is for your honesty.

FIRST WATCH If we know him to be a thief, shall we not lay hands on him?

DOGBERRY   Truly, by your office you may, but I think they that touch pitch will be defiled. The most peaceable way for you, if you do take a thief, is to let him show himself what he is and steal out of your company.   **45**

VERGES   You have been always called a merciful man, partner.

DOGBERRY   Truly, I would not hang a dog by my will, much more a man who hath any honesty in him.

VERGES   If you hear a child cry in the night, you must call to the nurse and bid her still it.   **50**

SECOND WATCH How if the nurse be asleep and will not hear us?

DOGBERRY   Why then, depart in peace and let the child wake her with crying; for the ewe that will not hear her lamb when it baes will never answer a calf when he bleats.

56   *present* (for *represent*)

57   *stay* detain, stop

59   *'a* he

60   *Five shillings to one on't* I'll bet five shillings to one that he can (i.e. stop the Prince)
statutes laws

61   *Marry* a common exclamation

64   *By'r lady* i.e. By Our Lady, a common oath referring to the Virgin Mary

65–6   *of weight chances* of importance happens

66   *Keep … and your own* keep your official and private affairs secret

72   *coil* bustle, activity
vigitant (for *vigilant*)

74   *Peace; stir not* Be quiet; don't move

77   *Mass* by the Mass (a common oath)
my elbow itched (thought to be a warning against bad company).
scab as the result of scratching the itch; a rogue, villain

78   *I will owe thee an answer for that* I'll pay you back later for that insult
forward hurry up

79   *penthouse* overhanging roof

80   *like a true drunkard* refers to the Latin *in vino veritas* (wine brings out the truth): a drunkard won't guard his tongue but will tell the truth
utter all tell everything

81   *yet stand close* still stay hidden

83   *dear* expensive; valuable

86   *make* demand

87   *I wonder at it* I'm amazed

88   *unconfirmed* inexperienced

89   *is nothing to a man* shows nothing of the real man

90   *apparel* clothes

VERGES	'Tis very true.	55

DOGBERRY   This is the end of the charge: you, constable, are to present the
    Prince's own person. If you meet the Prince in the night, you may stay
    him.

VERGES   Nay, by'r lady, that I think 'a cannot.

DOGBERRY   Five shillings to one on't, with any man that knows the statutes,   60
    he may stay him. Marry, not without the prince be willing, for indeed
    the watch ought to offend no man, and it is an offence to stay a man
    against his will.

VERGES   By'r lady, I think it be so.

DOGBERRY   Ha, ah ha! Well, masters, good-night; an there be any matter of   65
    weight chances, call up me. Keep your fellows' counsels and your own,
    and good-night. Come, neighbour.

SECOND WATCH Well, masters, we hear our charge. Let us go sit here upon the
    church bench till two, and then all to bed.

DOGBERRY [*Coming back*] One word more, honest neighbours: I pray you   70
    watch about Signor Leonato's door, for the wedding being there
    tomorrow, there is a great coil tonight. Adieu. Be vigitant, I beseech you.

[*Exeunt* DOGBERRY *and* VERGES

Enter BORACHIO *and* CONRADE

BORACHIO   What, Conrade?

SECOND WATCH [*Aside*] Peace; stir not.

BORACHIO   Conrade, I say!   75

CONRADE   Here, man, I am at thy elbow.

BORACHIO   Mass, and my elbow itched; I thought there would a scab follow.

CONRADE   I will owe thee an answer for that; and now forward with thy tale.

BORACHIO   Stand thee close then under this penthouse, for it drizzles rain, and
    I will, like a true drunkard, utter all to thee.   80

SECOND WATCH [*Aside*] Some treason, masters; yet stand close.

BORACHIO   Therefore know, I have earned of Don John a thousand ducats.

CONRADE   Is it possible that any villainy should be so dear?

BORACHIO   Thou shouldst rather ask if it were possible any villainy should be
    so rich; for when rich villains have need of poor ones, poor ones may   85
    make what price they will.

CONRADE   I wonder at it.

BORACHIO   That shows thou art unconfirmed; thou knowest that the fashion
    of a doublet, or a hat, or a cloak, is nothing to a man.

CONRADE   Yes, it is apparel.   90

BORACHIO   I mean the fashion.

CONRADE   Yes, the fashion is the fashion.

93 *Tush!* Rubbish!

94 *deformed thief* warped robber (of common sense)

95 *Deformed* The Second Watch has heard Borachio mention the word *thief* and thinks he means an actual thief called *Deformed*, whom the Watch now claims to know.

98 *vane* weather vane

101 *fashioning them like* making them like
Pharaoh King of Egypt who pursued the Israelites and was drowned with his soldiers in the Red Sea (Exodus Chapter 14 verses 23–8)

102 *reechy* discoloured by smoke

102–3 *god Bel's priests in the old church window* In the Bible the priests of Bel were overthrown by King Cyrus when Daniel revealed that they were imposing a false god on the people (Daniel Chapter 14 verses 1–22). The story was sometimes depicted in the stained glass windows of churches.

103 *shaven Hercules* The Greek hero, Hercules, was dressed as a woman and made to carry out menial tasks – but Borachio may be confusing him with the Bible story of Samson who was enslaved by his enemies when his long hair was cut by his mistress, Delilah (Judges Chapter 16 verses 1–31). *smirched* besmirched, dirtied

104 *cod-piece* the pouch at the front of a man's breeches: originally they gave support rather like modern underwear but later became largely decorative and exaggeratedly prominent, as in Borachio's account. *massy* massive

105–6 *the fashion … the man* clothes are discarded not because they are worn out but because the fashion has changed

112 *possessed* informed

> How would you stage the Borachio/Conrade episode? Look for clues in the text.
> * How do the Watch members react to what they hear?
> * How would you manage the arrest: would there be a (comic?) scuffle?

123 *stand* halt

124 *right* an honorary title, as 'right honourable'. *recovered* (for *discovered*)

125 lechery (for *treachery*)

126 *a lock* a lock of hair called a love-lock, grown by the left ear

128 *warrant* guarantee

130 *obey* (for *order*)

131 *a goodly commodity* fine goods. *taken up* arrested; bought on credit

132 *bills* bonds of sale; weapons (see line 31)

133 *in question* in demand or sought after; subject to legal questioning; of questionable (i.e. doubtful) value

> Compare the effect of this scene with those that come immediately before and after: here the plot initiated at the end of Act 3 Scene 2 by Don John has been successfully carried out; the Watch have heard the details of the plot and arrested the culprits – but are we wholly reassured? Meanwhile Hero joyfully prepares for the wedding (Act 3 Scene 3) unaware of what lies ahead.
>
> How is Shakespeare manipulating the feelings and expectations of his audience?

Dogberry pompously gives confused orders for the conduct of the Watch, instructing them to pay particular attention to Leonato's house. Borachio drunkenly boasts to Conrade of his success in convincing Claudio and Don Pedro of Hero's disloyalty. The Watch arrest the offenders.

BORACHIO   Tush! I may as well say the fool's the fool. But see'st thou not what a deformed thief this fashion is?

SECOND WATCH [*Aside*] I know that Deformed; 'a has been a vile thief this seven   95
year; 'a goes up and down like a gentleman. I remember his name.

BORACHIO   Didst thou not hear somebody?

CONRADE   No, 'twas the vane on the house.

BORACHIO   Seest thou not, I say, what a deformed thief this fashion is? How
giddily 'a turns about all the hot-bloods, between fourteen and five-and-   100
thirty – sometimes fashioning them like Pharaoh's soldiers in the
reechy painting, sometime like god Bel's priests in the old church
window, sometime like the shaven Hercules in the smirched worm-
eaten tapestry, where his cod-piece seems as massy as his club?

CONRADE   All this I see, and I see that the fashion wears out more apparel   105
than the man. But art not thou thyself giddy with the fashion too, that
thou hast shifted out of thy tale into telling me of the fashion?

BORACHIO   Not so, neither; but know that I have tonight wooed Margaret, the
Lady Hero's gentle-woman, by the name of Hero. She leans me out at
her mistress' chamber window, bids me a thousand times good-night –   110
I tell this tale vilely – I should first tell thee how the Prince, Claudio,
and my master, planted and placed and possessed by my master, Don
John, saw afar off in the orchard this amiable encounter.

CONRADE   And thought they Margaret was Hero?

BORACHIO   Two of them did, the Prince and Claudio; but the devil my master   115
knew she was Margaret; and partly by his oaths, which first possessed
them, partly by the dark night, which did deceive them, but chiefly by
my villainy, which did confirm any slander that Don John had made,
away went Claudio enraged – swore he would meet her as he was
appointed next morning at the temple; and there, before the whole   120
congregation, shame her with what he saw o'er night, and send her
home again without a husband.

The WATCH *come forward excitedly*

SECOND WATCH We charge you in the Prince's name, stand!

FIRST WATCH Call up the right Master Constable. We have here recovered the most
dangerous piece of lechery that ever was known in the commonwealth.   125

SECOND WATCH And one Deformed is one of them; I know him, 'a wears a lock.

CONRADE   Masters, masters –

FIRST WATCH You'll be made bring Deformed forth, I warrant you.

CONRADE   Masters –

SECOND WATCH Never speak, we charge you; let us obey you to go with us.   130

BORACHIO   We are like to prove a goodly commodity, being taken up of these
men's bills.

CONRADE   A commodity in question, I warrant you. Come, we'll obey you.

[*Exeunt*

3:4

As Hero chooses clothing for her wedding the conversation turns to men and sexual banter. When Beatrice enters, her cold provides the occasion for much good-natured teasing about her love for Benedick.

4 *Well* Right away

5 *Troth* in truth. *rebato* a stiff ornamental collar or ruff

6 *Meg* a familiar name for Margaret

9 *new tire within* new head-dress inside the house. *a thought* a shade

10 *a most rare fashion* very refined indeed

12 *that exceeds* that's better than any

13 *'s but a night-gown* it's only a dressing-gown
cloth o' gold a rich fabric with gold thread woven into it

14 *cuts* slits to show other fabrics underneath. *laced* embroidered
down-sleeves sleeves close-fitting at the wrist

14–15 *side-sleeves* long loose sleeves hanging from the shoulder

15 *round underborne* trimmed round the hem

16 *quaint* stylish. *on't* of it

19 *Fie* an exclamation expressing shock

20 *honourably* honestly

21 *in a beggar* even for a beggar. *without marriage* without being married

21–2 *I think … a husband* Margaret is teasing Hero by claiming to think that she is being too coy in being shocked at Margaret's earlier reference to a *man*. She wonders whether she would have been less offended if she had used the word *husband*.

22 *saving your reverence* an expression of respect or apology (here used mischievously). *an* if

23 *wrest* twist

24–5 *an it be … right wife* as long as they are lawfully married to one another, i.e. not somebody else's husband or wife!

25 *light* immoral

Many productions have used Beatrice's cold for comic business. How could you introduce comedy into the scene: costume: (dressing gown, blanket, slippers); coughs and sneezes (is her speech affected by her cold?); treatment (inhaling, pills, medicine)?

How does Beatrice react to Margaret's teasing about her love for Benedick – is she in the mood for jokes?

29 *sick tune* melancholy mood

31 *Clap's* clap us (i.e. clap the beat)
that goes without a burden that can be sung without a bass line

33 *Ye light … your heels* you dance the tune; you're *light* (i.e. unchaste) in matters of love

33–4 *have stables enough* i.e. is rich enough; is sufficiently well-endowed (i.e. sexually)

34 *barns* puns on the previous reference to stables and 'bairns' (i.e. children)

35 *illegitimate construction* false interpretation, also punning on the idea of *illegitimate* children

37 *Heigh-ho!* Beatrice sighs. She had used the same expression earlier (Act 2 Scene 1 line 239). Then it was used in jest; now it's genuine. 'Heigh' was also used as a cry of encouragement to a horse or hawk, hence Margaret's remark (line 38).

3:4   *Enter* Hero *with* Margaret *and* Ursula

Hero	Good Ursula, wake my cousin Beatrice and desire her to rise.
Ursula	I will, lady.
Hero	And bid her come hither.
Ursula	Well.

[*Exit*

Margaret	Troth, I think your other rebato were better.	**5**
Hero	No, pray thee good Meg, I'll wear this.	
Margaret	By my troth, 's not so good; and I warrant your cousin will say so.	
Hero	My cousin's a fool, and thou art another. I'll wear none but this.	
Margaret	I like the new tire within excellently, if the hair were a thought browner; and your gown's a most rare fashion, i'faith. I saw the Duchess of Milan's gown that they praise so.	**10**
Hero	O that exceeds, they say.	
Margaret	By my troth, 's but a night-gown in respect of yours – cloth o' gold and cuts, and laced with silver, set with pearls, down-sleeves, side-sleeves, and skirts, round underborne with a bluish tinsel; but for a fine, quaint, graceful and excellent fashion, yours is worth ten on't.	**15**
Hero	God give me joy to wear it, for my heart is exceeding heavy.	
Margaret	'Twill be heavier soon, by the weight of a man.	
Hero	Fie upon thee; art not ashamed?	
Margaret	Of what, lady? Of speaking honourably? Is not marriage honourable in a beggar? Is not your lord honourable without marriage? I think you would have me say 'saving your reverence, a husband'; an bad thinking do not wrest true speaking, I'll offend nobody. Is there any harm in 'the heavier for a husband'? None, I think, an it be the right husband and the right wife; otherwise 'tis light and not heavy. Ask my Lady Beatrice else – here she comes.	**20** **25**

Enter Beatrice

Hero	Good morrow, coz.	
Beatrice	Good morrow, sweet Hero.	
Hero	Why, how now? Do you speak in the sick tune?	
Beatrice	I am out of all other tune, methinks.	**30**
Margaret	Clap's into 'Light o' love' – that goes without a burden. Do you sing it and I'll dance it.	
Beatrice	Ye light o' love with your heels! Then if your husband have stables enough, you'll see he shall lack no barns.	
Margaret	O illegitimate construction! I scorn that with my heels.	**35**
Beatrice	'Tis almost five o'clock, cousin; 'tis time you were ready. By my troth, I am exceeding ill. Heigh-ho!	

39 *H* The word 'Ache' used to be pronounced 'Aitch'. Beatrice puns on the word.

40 *an you be not turned Turk* if you have not changed your faith (by falling in love). Beatrice had always previously maintained her 'faith' in not succumbing to love.

40–1 *there's no more sailing by the star* Sailors always used the Pole Star as an absolutely reliable reference point for navigation. If Beatrice has fallen in love then nothing is certain any more; even the Pole Star can't be relied upon.

42 *trow* I wonder

45 *I am stuffed* i.e. stuffed up with a head cold

46 *A maid and stuffed!* Margaret picks up the vulgar pun; *stuffed* could also mean 'pregnant'.
There's goodly That's a fine result

47–8 *professed apprehension* claimed to be witty

49 *become me rarely* suit me well

50 *wear it in your cap* i.e. show it more noticeably

52 *Carduus Benedictus* a herb known as the 'blessed thistle' which was thought to be a powerful cure-all. Here Margaret puns on Benedick's name in prescribing a medicine for Beatrice's illness.

53 *qualm* sudden sickness

54 *There … thistle* i.e. you've touched a sore point (with a crude pun on *prick*)

55 *moral* hidden

58 *perchance* perhaps

59 *by'r lady* by Our Lady (i.e. the Virgin Mary), a common mild oath. *list* please

60 *if I would* even if I could

62 *such another* just like that

62–3 *is he become a man* he has become a real man (by falling in love)

64 *eats his meat without grudging* accepts his fate (i.e. to marry) without complaining.
may be might be; could have been

65–6 *you look … other women do* i.e. Beatrice is no different from other women in having an eye for men. The eye was also considered the agent of passion.

68 *false gallop* canter. This is a taught step not a natural step for a horse. Margaret means that what she says is the truth.

69 *withdraw* i.e. to dress for the wedding

70 *gallants* young men

Before this scene Margaret has spoken only one line (Act 3 Scene 1 line 14) yet she has played a vital off-stage role as 'Hero' in Don John's plot. Compare her light-hearted sexual repartee here with the dreadful consequences in Act 4 Scene 1 of her casual sexual liaison with Borachio.

Margaret helps Hero prepare for the wedding and teases her with witty allusions to the wedding night. With Beatrice's arrival the taunting changes direction to focus on her changed attitude to both marriage and Benedick. Hero exits to dress for the wedding.

MARGARET	For a hawk, a horse, or a husband?
BEATRICE	For the letter that begins them all, H.
MARGARET	Well, an you be not turned Turk, there's no more sailing by the **40** star.
BEATRICE	What means the fool, trow?
MARGARET	Nothing I; but God send everyone their heart's desire!
HERO	These gloves the Count sent me; they are an excellent perfume.
BEATRICE	I am stuffed, cousin; I cannot smell. **45**
MARGARET	A maid and stuffed! There's goodly catching of cold.
BEATRICE	O, God help me, God help me! How long have you professed apprehension?
MARGARET	Ever since you left it. Doth not my wit become me rarely?
BEATRICE	It is not seen enough; you should wear it in your cap. By my troth, I **50** am sick.
MARGARET	Get you some of this distilled Carduus Benedictus and lay it to your heart; it is the only thing for a qualm.
HERO	There thou prickest her with a thistle.
BEATRICE	Benedictus? Why Benedictus? You have some moral in this **55** Benedictus?
MARGARET	Moral? No, by my troth, I have no moral meaning; I mean plain holy-thistle. You may think perchance that I think you are in love? Nay, by'r lady, I am not such a fool to think what I list, nor I list not to think what I can; nor indeed I cannot think, if I would think my heart out of **60** thinking, that you are in love, or that you will be in love, or that you can be in love. Yet Benedick was such another, and now is he become a man; he swore he would never marry, and yet now, in despite of his heart, he eats his meat without grudging. And how you may be concerted, I know not; but methinks you look with your eyes as other **65** women do.
BEATRICE	What pace is this that thy tongue keeps?
MARGARET	Not a false gallop.

Enter URSULA

URSULA	Madam, withdraw. The Prince, the Count, Signor Benedick, Don John and all the gallants of the town are come to fetch you to church. **70**
HERO	Help to dress me, good coz, good Meg, good Ursula.

[*Exeunt*

3:5

Leonato is busy with the final wedding preparations when Dogberry and Verges come to tell him of the arrest of Borachio and Conrade. However, he finds their ramblings incomprehensible and tells Dogberry to conduct the trial himself.

1	*would you* do you want
2	*confidence* (for *conference*). *decerns* (for concerns)
3	*nearly* personally
8	*off the matter* off the point, irrelevantly
9	*blunt* (for *sharp*)
10	*as the skin … brows* Dogberry probably means 'between his eyebrows'. The forehead generally was regarded as an indicator of character, if accurately interpreted; honesty was particularly revealed between the eyebrows.
13	*odorous* (for *odious*). *palabras* Dogberry's version of '*pocas palabras*', Spanish for 'few words', a popular expression at the time
16	*tedious* long-winded
16–17	Dogberry seems to think *tedious* means 'rich'.
19	*and 'twere* even if it was
20	*exclamation on* complaint against (probably for *acclamation of*)
23	*fain* gladly
25	*ha' ta'en* have arrested. *arrant* complete
26–7	*'When the age is in … out'* Dogberry mistakes the proverb 'When ale is in, wit is out'.

In making the most of his moment of glory Dogberry generates both comedy and acute suspense through his self-important report of the arrest. How might this be shown on stage?

- *How do Dogberry and Verges behave towards Leonato – with exaggerated courtesy?*
- *Is there some rivalry between Dogberry and Verges – how might this be shown on stage?*
- *How does Leonato react – bewildered, irritable, exasperated, trying to be patient, is he still dressing?*
- *Is there the bustle of last-minute wedding preparations: guests, flowers, off-stage music?*

27	*it is a world to see* what a world we live in
28	*God's a good man* i.e. God is good (proverbial)
28–9	*an two men … behind* Dogberry thinks it is a sign of God's fairness that he has made himself superior to Verges.
32	*comes too short of you* falls short of you
35	*comprehended* (for *apprehended*)
36	*aspicious* (for *suspicious*)
39	*as it may appear unto you* as you can see

3:5   *Enter* LEONATO, DOGBERRY *and* VERGES

LEONATO	What would you with me, honest neighbour?
DOGBERRY	Marry, sir, I would have some confidence with you, that decerns you nearly.
LEONATO	Brief, I pray you, for you see it is a busy time with me.
DOGBERRY	Marry, this it is, sir.

DOGBERRY   Marry, this it is, sir.   5

VERGES   Yes, in truth it is, sir.

LEONATO   What is it, my good friends?

DOGBERRY   Goodman Verges, sir, speaks a little off the matter – an old man,
sir, and his wits are not so blunt as, God help, I would desire they were;
but, in faith, honest, as the skin between his brows.   10

VERGES   Yes, I thank God, I am as honest as any man living that is an old
man and no honester than I.

DOGBERRY   Comparisons are odorous; *palabras*, neighbour Verges.

LEONATO   Neighbours, you are tedious.

DOGBERRY   It pleases your worship to say so, but we are the poor Duke's   15
officers. But truly for mine own part, if I were as tedious as a king, I
could find in my heart to bestow it all of your worship.

LEONATO   All thy tediousness on me, ah?

DOGBERRY   Yea, and 'twere a thousand pound more than 'tis, for I hear as good
exclamation on your worship as of any man in the city, and though I be   20
but a poor man, I am glad to hear it.

VERGES   And so am I.

LEONATO   I would fain know what you have to say.

VERGES   Marry, sir, our watch tonight, excepting your worship's presence,
ha' ta'en a couple of as arrant knaves as any in Messina.   25

DOGBERRY   A good old man, sir, he will be talking; as they say, 'When the age
is in, the wit is out'. God help us, it is a world to see! Well said i'faith,
neighbour Verges; well, God's a good man, an two men ride of a horse,
one must ride behind. An honest soul i'faith, sir, by my troth he is, as
ever broke bread. But – God is to be worshipped – all men are not alike;   30
alas, good neighbour!

LEONATO   Indeed, neighbour, he comes too short of you.

DOGBERRY   Gifts that God gives.

LEONATO   I must leave you.

DOGBERRY   One word, sir. Our watch, sir, have indeed comprehended two   35
aspicious persons, and we would have them this morning examined
before your worship.

LEONATO   Take their examination yourself, and bring it me. I am now in great
haste, as it may appear unto you.

40 *suffigance* (for *sufficient*)

42 *stay* are waiting

43 *wait* attend

45 *inkhorn* horn holding ink, often worn at the waist
examination examine

47 *spare for no wit* bestow all our attention on it; won't waste any
intelligence on it. Again Dogberry unconsciously ridicules himself.

48 *non-come* Dogberry's version of *non compos mentis* (i.e. insane)

49 *excommunication* (for *examination*)

In this scene it is ironic that Leonato's anxiety about the wedding causes him
not to realise the full significance of the interview. Compare this scene with
other episodes in the play when those involved understand only part of the
truth, either through misunderstanding or misrepresentation.

---

*Last-minute preparations for the wedding preoccupy Leonato so that when
Dogberry and Verges report the arrest of Borachio and Conrade he becomes
impatient with their confused story and does not realise the significance of the
crime that they describe.*

DOGBERRY	It shall be suffigance.	**40**
LEONATO	Drink some wine ere you go; fare you well.	

Enter a MESSENGER

MESSENGER My lord, they stay for you, to give your daughter to her husband.

LEONATO I'll wait upon them; I am ready.

[*Exeunt* LEONATO *and* MESSENGER

DOGBERRY Go, good partner, go get you to Francis Seacoal; bid him bring his pen and inkhorn to the gaol. We are now to examination these men. **45**

VERGES And we must do it wisely.

DOGBERRY We will spare for no wit, I warrant you. Here's that shall drive some of them to a non-come; only get the learned writer, to set down our excommunication, and meet me at the gaol.

[*Exeunt*

4:1

As the wedding ceremony begins Claudio denounces Hero publicly. Hero's pleas of innocence are brushed aside and she faints. When her accusers have left and Hero begins to recover she is violently berated by her father but the Friar reveals a plan to restore Claudio's love. Alone at last, Beatrice and Benedick confirm their mutual love and Benedick agrees to challenge Claudio.

Leonato's request for **the plain form of marriage** (line 1) suggests simple staging in the Renaissance theatre. Why would some ceremonial be dramatically effective? How might you create appropriate formality: setting, processions, costumes, stage dressing, music?

'You come hither, my lord, to marry this lady?'

8 *inward* secret
16 *interjections* a term from formal grammar books referring to expressions of emotion (such as Claudio's line 14)
16–17 *ah, ha, he!* Benedick offers further examples of grammatical *interjections*
18 *Stand thee by* stand aside
    Father i.e. Leonato – ironic as Leonato was expecting to become Claudio's father-in-law

---

Don Pedro had played an important part in making possible the marriage of Claudio and Hero. Compare his role in Claudio's rejection of Hero. Can you find evidence that Claudio and the Prince had colluded to 'stage' the rejection? Does that affect your view of them?

---

24 *render her again* give her back again
27 *rotten orange* i.e. whore. The image suggests something that looks appealing but which is corrupt within. Venereal disease was also known as 'the rot'.
28 *but the sign and semblance* only the outward appearance and imitation
32 *that blood as modest evidence* her blush as proof of her chastity
33 *To witness* as a witness in support of
36 *heat of a luxurious bed* passion of a lustful bed

4:1   *Enter* DON PEDRO, DON JOHN, LEONATO, FRIAR, CLAUDIO,
BENEDICK, HERO, BEATRICE *and* ATTENDANTS

LEONATO   Come Friar Francis, be brief – only to the plain form of marriage,
and you shall recount their particular duties afterwards.

FRIAR   You come hither, my lord, to marry this lady?

CLAUDIO   No.

LEONATO   To be married to her, Friar; you come to marry her!   5

FRIAR   Lady, you come hither to be married to this Count?

HERO   I do.

FRIAR   If either of you know any inward impediment why you should not
be conjoined, I charge you on your souls to utter it.

CLAUDIO   Know you any, Hero?   10

HERO   None, my lord.

FRIAR   Know you any, Count?

LEONATO   I dare make his answer – none.

CLAUDIO   O, what men dare do! What men may do!
What men daily do, not knowing what they do!   15

BENEDICK   How now – interjections? Why then, some be of laughing, as ah,
ha, he!

CLAUDIO   Stand thee by, Friar. Father, by your leave,
Will you with free and unconstrainèd soul
Give me this maid, your daughter?   20

LEONATO   As freely, son, as God did give her me.

He places her hand in CLAUDIO'S

CLAUDIO   And what have I to give you back, whose worth
May counterpoise this rich and precious gift?

DON PEDRO   Nothing, unless you render her again.

CLAUDIO   Sweet Prince, you learn me noble thankfulness.   25
There, Leonato, take her back again.
Give not this rotten orange to your friend;
She's but the sign and semblance of her honour.
Behold, how like a maid she blushes here!
O, what authority and show of truth   30
Can cunning sin cover itself withal!
Comes not that blood as modest evidence
To witness simple virtue? Would you not swear,
All you that see her, that she were a maid
By these exterior shows? But she is none.   35
She knows the heat of a luxurious bed;
Her blush is guiltiness, not modesty.

39 *approvèd wanton* proven whore

40 *in your own proof* in testing her virtue yourself

43 *known her* had sexual intercourse with her

45 *extenuate the 'forehand sin* excuse the sin of anticipating the wedding
'forehand beforehand

47 *large* tempting, persuasive

49 *comely* proper, appropriate

51 *Out on thee seeming!* to hell with your seeming
write against it formally denounce you

52 *Dian* The Moon goddess, Diana, was the goddess of Chastity.
orb course

53 *blown* in full bloom

54 *more intemperate in your blood* more immoderate in your sensual appetites, i.e. promiscuous

55 *Venus* goddess of Love. *pampered* unrestrained

56 *That rage in savage sensuality* that are crazed by untamed sensual instincts

Some productions have represented Claudio's denunciation of Hero as vicious and brutal; others have softened his rejection and created a more sympathetic character. Try out different readings of his lines up to line 56 to invite different audience responses.

Things to work on:

- *Tone of voice: hard, unemotional, venomous, savage or gentle, full of sadness and regret (look at lines 47–9)?*
- *How does he look at Hero?*
- *Does he physically touch Hero?*

57 *so wide* so wildly, out of control

59 *that have* (I) who have

60 *stale* prostitute

69 *that fatherly and kindly power* by your natural authority as a father (*kindly* = natural)

72 *beset* attacked from all sides

73 *catechising* questioning. The catechism is a series of questions on the Christian faith learned before confirmation. Here it seems to Hero that she is being interrogated to see whether she is fit to receive the sacrament of marriage.

74 *to your name* Hero's name represented faithfulness in love, after the classical Greek story of Hero and Leander. Leander was drowned as he tried to swim the Hellespont to meet Hero and she drowned herself for love of him. The question 'What is your name?' was also the first question in the catechism.

75 *blot* stain

76 *just reproach* justifiable criticism

LEONATO   What do you mean, my lord?

CLAUDIO   Not to be married,
     Not to knit my soul to an approvèd wanton.

LEONATO   Dear my lord, if you in your own proof   **40**
     Have vanquished the resistance of her youth,
     And made defeat of her virginity –

CLAUDIO   I know what you would say. If I have known her,
     You will say she did embrace me as a husband,
     And so extenuate the 'forehand sin.   **45**
     No, Leonato,
     I never tempted her with word too large,
     But, as a brother to his sister, showed
     Bashful sincerity and comely love.

HERO   And seemed I ever otherwise to you?   **50**

CLAUDIO   Out on thee seeming! I will write against it:
     You seem to me as Dian in her orb,
     As chaste as in the bud ere it be blown.
     But you are more intemperate in your blood
     Than Venus, or those pampered animals   **55**
     That rage in savage sensuality.

HERO   Is my lord well, that he doth speak so wide?

LEONATO   Sweet Prince, why speak not you?

DON PEDRO   What should I speak?
     I stand dishonoured, that have gone about
     To link my dear friend to a common stale.   **60**

LEONATO   Are these things spoken, or do I but dream?

DON JOHN   Sir, they are spoken, and these things are true.

BENEDICK [*Aside*] This looks not like a nuptial.

HERO   True? O God!

CLAUDIO   Leonato, stand I here?
     Is this the Prince? Is this the Prince's brother?   **65**
     Is this face Hero's? Are our eyes our own?

LEONATO   All this is so, but what of this, my lord?

CLAUDIO   Let me but move one question to your daughter,
     And by that fatherly and kindly power
     That you have in her, bid her answer truly.   **70**

LEONATO   I charge thee do so, as thou art my child.

HERO   O God defend me, how am I beset!
     What kind of catechising call you this?

CLAUDIO   To make you answer truly to your name.

HERO   Is it not Hero? Who can blot that name   **75**
     With any just reproach?

76 *Marry* Claudio's use of this common exclamation seems particularly ironic in the present circumstances. *that can Hero* i.e. her very name is a *blot*

80 *answer to this* explain that away

84 *grievèd* wronged (because his honour is threatened)

87 *liberal* depraved

90 *Fie, fie* an expression of strong horror and disgust

92–3 *There is not … utter them* one gives offence even in uttering the words to name her actions

94 *misgovernment* misconduct

95 *what a Hero* Claudio possibly compares Hero bitterly with her classical namesake

96–7 *If half … heart* if half of your physical beauty had gone to make pure your mind and feelings

99 *impiety* wickedness

100 *For thee* because of what you have done to me
the gates of love the senses which give love access. Of all the senses that of sight was considered the most powerful stimulus to love.

101 *conjecture* suspicion

102 *To turn … harm* i.e. from now on his eyes will interpret all forms of beauty as being potentially harmful

103 *more* again
gracious delightful

106 *these things* i.e. her sinful deeds

107 *Smother her spirits up* overwhelm her vital powers

What part does Margaret play in this scene? How much did she know about Don John's plot to shame Hero? Did Borachio tell her it was a joke? Did she know anything?

- Was she one of Hero's bridesmaids?
- At what points might she suspect and finally realise the full significance of her misdeed?
- Could she instinctively want to intervene to explain – and would Don John be watchful for her reaction? Might he prevent it?
- What might be her reaction? Would she exit – at what point?

110 *take not away thy heavy hand* Leonato suggests that if Hero has sunk down under the weight of her shame, God should not now intervene since death would be the most suitable way to shroud her disgrace.

CLAUDIO	Marry, that can Hero:	

CLAUDIO   Marry, that can Hero:
   Hero itself can blot out Hero's virtue.
   What man was he talked with you yesternight,
   Out at your window betwixt twelve and one?
   Now, if you are a maid, answer to this.   80

HERO   I talked with no man at that hour, my lord.

DON PEDRO Why, then are you no maiden. Leonato,
   I am sorry you must hear. Upon mine honour,
   Myself, my brother, and this grievèd Count
   Did see her, hear her, at that hour last night 85
   Talk with a ruffian at her chamber window;
   Who hath indeed, most like a liberal villain,
   Confessed the vile encounters they have had
   A thousand times in secret.

DON JOHN Fie, fie, they are not to be named, my lord, 90
   Not to be spoke of!
   There is not chastity enough in language
   Without offence to utter them. Thus, pretty lady,
   I am sorry for thy much misgovernment.

CLAUDIO O Hero, what a Hero hadst thou been, 95
   If half thy outward graces had been placed
   About thy thoughts and counsels of thy heart!
   But fare thee well, most foul, most fair; farewell
   Thou pure impiety, and impious purity!
   For thee I'll lock up all the gates of love 100
   And on my eyelids shall conjecture hang,
   To turn all beauty into thoughts of harm,
   And never shall it more be gracious.

LEONATO Hath no man's dagger here a point for me?

        HERO *collapses*

BEATRICE Why how now, cousin, wherefore sink you down? 105

DON JOHN Come, let us go; these things, come thus to light,
   Smother her spirits up.
        [*Exeunt* DON PEDRO, DON JOHN *and* CLAUDIO

BENEDICK How doth the lady?

BEATRICE   Dead, I think – help, uncle!
   Hero? Why, Hero! Uncle! Signor Benedick! Friar!

LEONATO O Fate, take not away thy heavy hand! 110
   Death is the fairest cover for her shame
   That may be wished for.

BEATRICE   How now, cousin Hero?

       HERO *begins to revive*

114 *wherefore* why

117 *printed in her blood* confirmed by her blushes

119 *did I think* if I thought

120 *thy spirits* your physical powers

121 *on the rearward of reproaches* as the sequel to my censure of you

122 *Grieved I, I had but one?* Did I really mourn the fact that I had only one child?

123 *Chid I … frame?* Did I really reproach nature for being so meagre?

124 *one too much by thee* you have made it one too many (i.e. children)

126 *with charitable hand* as an act of charity

127 *issue* child

128 *smirchèd thus … infamy* tarnished and soiled by disgrace as she is now

133 *That I myself … mine* my own welfare took second place to hers

134 *Valuing of her* so highly did I esteem her

137–8 *And salt too little … tainted flesh!* Leonato compares Hero's disgraced body (*tainted flesh*) with meat that has gone bad. Salt would be used to both preserve meat and disguise its tainted flavour when it was no longer fresh. In Hero's case all the salt found in the sea wouldn't be able to disguise (*season*) the corruption of her body.

139 *attired in wonder* covered in amazement

141 *belied* slandered, accused falsely

142 *Lady, were you her bedfellow last night?* It was common for adults of the same sex to share a bed.

145 *that* i.e. the evidence against Hero

148 *that speaking* that while speaking

153 *By noting of the lady* in order to observe her

154 *blushing apparitions* signs of blushing

155 *innocent shames* looks of outraged modesty

FRIAR	Have comfort, lady.
LEONATO	Dost thou look up?
FRIAR	Yea, wherefore should she not?

LEONATO   Wherefore? Why, doth not every earthly thing   **115**
　　　　　Cry shame upon her? Could she here deny
　　　　　The story that is printed in her blood?
　　　　　Do not live, Hero, do not ope thine eyes.
　　　　　For did I think thou wouldst not quickly die,
　　　　　Thought I thy spirits were strong than thy shames,   **120**
　　　　　Myself would – on the rearward of reproaches –
　　　　　Strike at thy life. Grieved I, I had but one?
　　　　　Chid I for that at frugal Nature's frame?
　　　　　O, one too much by thee; why had I one?
　　　　　Why ever wast thou lovely in my eyes?   **125**
　　　　　Why had I not with charitable hand
　　　　　Took up a beggar's issue at my gates,
　　　　　Who smirchèd thus and mired with infamy,
　　　　　I might have said, 'No part of it is mine;
　　　　　This shame derives itself from unknown loins'?   **130**
　　　　　But mine, and mine I loved, and mine I praised,
　　　　　And mine that I was proud on, mine so much
　　　　　That I myself was to myself not mine,
　　　　　Valuing of her – why she, O she is fall'n
　　　　　Into a pit of ink, that the wide sea   **135**
　　　　　Hath drops too few to wash her clean again,
　　　　　And salt too little which may season give
　　　　　To her foul tainted flesh!

BENEDICK   Sir, sir, be patient.
　　　　　For my part, I am so attired in wonder,
　　　　　I know not what to say.   **140**

BEATRICE   O, on my soul, my cousin is belied!

BENEDICK   Lady, were you her bedfellow last night?

BEATRICE   No, truly, not, although until last night
　　　　　I have this twelvemonth been her bedfellow.

LEONATO   Confirmed, confirmed! O, that is stronger made,   **145**
　　　　　Which was before barred up with ribs of iron!
　　　　　Would the two Princes lie? And Claudio lie –
　　　　　Who loved her so, that speaking of her foulness,
　　　　　Washed it with tears? Hence from her – let her die!

FRIAR   Hear me a little;   **150**
　　　　　For I have only silent been so long,
　　　　　And given way unto this course of fortune,
　　　　　By noting of the lady. I have marked
　　　　　A thousand blushing apparitions
　　　　　To start into her face, a thousand innocent shames   **155**

160   *reading* book learning (as opposed to worldly experience)

161–2   *Which with experimental … my book* i.e. his observations of the activities of the world
have corroborated his theoretical knowledge and confirmed it as true (*experimental
seal* = the confirmation of experience; *warrant* = guarantee)

163   *My reverence, calling, nor divinity* the respect due to me as a priest, my vocation, nor
my theological knowledge

165   *some biting error* a mistake which gnaws at Hero's spirits

166   *grace* decency

168   *perjury* lying while under oath

169   *cover* conceal

170   *in proper nakedness* completely exposed

172   *I know none* I don't know who it could be; I don't know any man sexually

174   *warrant* authorise, allow

175   *Let all my sins lack mercy!* i.e. let my soul be damned
my father i.e. probably the Friar, as priest

Is Hero's **my father** (line 175) addressed to Leonato or the Friar? Has Leonato
abandoned his 'fatherly' role? Is a father's duty to comfort and protect his
daughter taken over by Hero's spiritual 'father', the Friar?

How would you present Leonato in this episode: self-pitying and cruel or
sensitive and dignified?

- *Does he distance himself physically? Does he comfort Hero – if so, how?*
- *Does he avoid looking at her – or address himself to her?*
- *What is his tone of voice – full of regret, disappointment, compassionate,
  accusatory, bitter?*
- *What does he regret: the loss of Hero's honour – or his own reputation?*

Look at how other characters react to Leonato's words.

177   *unmeet* improper

178   *change* exchange

179   *Refuse me* deny me absolution (if to the Friar); disown me (if to her father)

180   *misprision* misunderstanding

181   *the very bent of honour* honourable in the highest degree

183   *practice of it* the person behind it

184   *Whose spirits .. villainies* whose whole being labours to do wickedness

185   *I know not* I don't know what to think

187   *proudest* highest in rank

188   *Time hath not … blood of mine* I'm not so old

189   *invention* ingenuity

190   *made such havoc of my means* so destroyed my wealth

191   *Nor my bad life … friends* nor has my life been so wicked as to deprive me of friends

192   *awaked in such a kind* stirred up by such an issue

193   *policy of mind* ingenuity

194   *quit me of them throughly* avenge me fully on them (i.e. those who have slandered
Hero's honour)

196   *let my counsel sway you* be persuaded by my advice

198   *kept in* hidden

In angel whiteness beat away those blushes;
And in her eye there hath appeared a fire,
To burn the errors that these Princes hold
Against her maiden truth. Call me a fool;
Trust not my reading, nor my observations,   160
Which with experimental seal doth warrant
The tenor of my book; trust not my age,
My reverence, calling, nor divinity,
If this sweet lady lie not guiltless here,
Under some biting error.

LEONATO   Friar, it cannot be.   165
Thou seest that all the grace that she hath left
Is that she will not add to her damnation
A sin of perjury; she not denies it.
Why seek'st thou then to cover with excuse
That which appears in proper nakedness?   170

FRIAR   Lady, what man is he you are accused of?

HERO   They know that do accuse me; I know none.
If I know more of any man alive
Than that which maiden modesty doth warrant,
Let all my sins lack mercy! O my father,   175
Prove you that any man with me conversed
At hours unmeet, or that I yesternight
Maintained the change of words with any creature,
Refuse me, hate me, torture me to death!

FRIAR   There is some strange misprision in the Princes.   180

BENEDICK   Two of them have the very bent of honour
And if their wisdoms be misled in this,
The practice of it lives in John the Bastard
Whose spirits toil in frame of villainies.

LEONATO   I know not. If they speak but truth of her,   185
These hands shall tear her; if they wrong her honour,
The proudest of them shall well hear of it.
Time hath not yet so dried this blood of mine,
Nor age so eat up my invention,
Nor fortune made such havoc of my means,   190
Nor my bad life reft me so much of friends,
But they shall find, awaked in such a kind,
Both strength of limb and policy of mind,
Ability in means and choice of friends,
To quit me of them throughly.

FRIAR   Pause awhile,   195
And let my counsel sway you in this case.
Your daughter here the Princes left for dead;
Let her awhile be secretly kept in,

199   *publish it*   let it be known

200   *mourning ostentation*   a show of formal mourning

201   *monument*   vault, burial chamber

203   *appertain unto*   are fitting for

204   *become of*   result from

205   *well carried*   well sustained

206   *remorse*   pity, regret

207   *strange course*   strange course of action

208   *But on … birth*   but from this labour expect a better ending (*travail* implies both 'work'/'effort' and 'childbirth')

212   *Of every hearer*   by everyone who hears her story
it so falls out   it is the case

213   *to the worth*   for its rightful value

215   *rack the value*   extend the value (the metaphor refers to the instrument of torture on which the offender was stretched to extract a confession)

219   *Th'idea of her life*   the image of what she was like when alive

220   *study of imagination*   moments of contemplation

221   *every lovely organ of her life*   each lovely aspect of her being

222   *apparelled … habit*   i.e. appear more richly dressed

223   *moving-delicate*   touchingly graceful

224   *Into the eye and prospect of his soul*   within the scope of the view of his innermost self

225   *Than when she lived indeed*   than when she was actually alive

226   *liver*   The liver was thought to be the seat of the passions.

229   *success*   succeeding events

230–1   *Will fashion … likelihood*   will shape the outcome even more favourably than I have speculated (*event* = outcome)

232   *But if all aim but this be levelled false*   but even if all other aspects of my plan come to nothing

233   *supposition of*   belief in

234   *the wonder of her infamy*   the gossip provoked by her disgrace

235   *sort*   turn out

237   *reclusive*   withdrawn (i.e. as a nun)

240   *inwardness*   intimacy

242   *deal in this*   treat this

243–4   *As secretly … your body*   with as much prudence and integrity as between your own body and soul

	And publish it that she is dead indeed.	
	Maintain a mourning ostentation,	200
	And on your family's old monument	
	Hang mournful epitaphs and do all rites	
	That appertain unto a burial.	

LEONATO What shall become of this? What will this do?

FRIAR Marry, this, well carried, shall on her behalf 205
Change slander to remorse; that is some good.
But not for that dream I on this strange course,
But on this travail look for greater birth.
She dying, as it must be so maintained,
Upon the instant that she was accused, 210
Shall be lamented, pitied and excused
Of every hearer. For it so falls out
That what we have we prize not to the worth,
Whiles we enjoy it; but being lacked and lost
Why then we rack the value, then we find 215
The virtue that possession would not show us
Whiles it was ours. So will it fare with Claudio.
When he shall hear she died upon his words,
Th' idea of her life shall sweetly creep
Into his study of imagination; 220
And every lovely organ of her life
Shall come apparelled in more precious habit,
More moving-delicate and full of life,
Into the eye and prospect of his soul
Than when she lived indeed. Then shall he mourn, 225
If ever love had interest in his liver,
And wish he had not so accusèd her;
No, though he thought his accusation true.
Let this be so, and doubt not but success
Will fashion the event in better shape 230
Than I can lay it down in likelihood.
But if all aim but this be levelled false,
The supposition of the lady's death
Will quench the wonder of her infamy.
And if it sort not well, you may conceal her – 235
As best befits her wounded reputation –
In some reclusive and religious life,
Out of all eyes, tongues, minds and injuries.

BENEDICK Signor Leonato, let the Friar advise you;
And though you know my inwardness and love 240
Is very much unto the Prince and Claudio,
Yet, by mine honour, I will deal in this
As secretly and justly as your soul
Should with your body.

244–5 *Being that I flow in grief … lead me* Leonato suggests that at present he is so overwhelmed by grief that he has lost the power to make independent judgements and can easily be led to follow any proposal (*flow* = like someone carried helplessly along by a current of water)

246 *Presently away* let's go straight away

247 *For to strange … cure* a proverbial idea: 'A desperate disease must have a desperate remedy' (*strangely* = ingeniously; *strain* = make a great effort with)

249 *prolonged* postponed

'Lady Beatrice, have you wept all this while?'

252 *desire* want (Beatrice understands him to mean 'request')

255 *right her* exonerate her

257 *even* simple. *no such friend* no one to do that act of friendship

259 *office* role, responsibility

265 *Do not swear and eat it* Benedick has just sworn *By my sword*. Beatrice warns against taking such an oath in case he has to eat his words/his sword ('To eat one's words' was proverbial).

269 *With no sauce … to it* i.e. Benedick will not retract his declaration of love for Beatrice no matter how much he might be induced to withdraw his vow (*sauce* = appetising accompaniment to food to make it more tasty). *protest* swear

270 *Why then, God forgive me!* Beatrice begs forgiveness because she had nearly broken the convention that the woman should not take any initiative in matters of love.

272 *stayed me in a happy hour* stopped me at the right moment

This first meeting between Beatrice and Benedick as lovers takes place against a background of conflicting emotions. How should lines 277–8 be spoken?

- *Is Benedick's* **Come, bid me do anything for thee** *light-hearted or serious? Is he swaggering, excited, restrained but sincere – did he expect the reply she gives him?*
- *Is Beatrice testing Benedick's love – or seeking vengeance on Claudio – or both? Is she using love as a weapon? Is she only half serious?*
- *How does she speak: quietly and intensely; with bitterness and hatred; with deadly calm?*
- *Could silence be used to intensify the moment?*
- *Is Benedick shocked, appalled, incredulous, startled? Does he think she is serious? What is the tone of his reply?*
- *Do they embrace, move apart, hold hands?*

In pairs learn the few lines 275–80 and experiment with different ways of delivering the lines. Compare the result.

279 *deny* refuse

280 *Tarry* wait

LEONATO	Being that I flow in grief
	The smallest twine may lead me. 245
FRIAR	'Tis well consented. Presently away;
	For to strange sores strangely they strain the cure.
	Come, lady, die to live – this wedding-day
	Perhaps is but prolonged; have patience and endure.

[*Exeunt all but* **BEATRICE** *and* **BENEDICK**

BENEDICK Lady Beatrice, have you wept all this while? 250

BEATRICE Yea, and I will weep a while longer.

BENEDICK I will not desire that.

BEATRICE You have no reason; I do it freely.

BENEDICK Surely I do believe your fair cousin is wronged.

BEATRICE Ah, how much might the man deserve of me that would right her! 255

BENEDICK Is there any way to show such friendship?

BEATRICE A very even way, but no such friend.

BENEDICK May a man do it?

BEATRICE It is a man's office, but not yours.

BENEDICK I do love nothing in the world so well as you; is not that strange? 260

BEATRICE As strange as the thing I know not; it were as possible for me to say I loved nothing so well as you. But believe me not; and yet I lie not. I confess nothing, nor I deny nothing. I am sorry for my cousin.

BENEDICK By my sword, Beatrice, thou lovest me.

BEATRICE Do not swear and eat it. 265

BENEDICK I will swear by it that you love me, and I will make him eat it that says I love not you.

BEATRICE Will you not eat your word?

BENEDICK With no sauce that can be devised to it. I protest I love thee.

BEATRICE Why then, God forgive me! 270

BENEDICK What offence, sweet Beatrice?

BEATRICE You have stayed me in a happy hour; I was about to protest I loved you.

BENEDICK And do it with all thy heart.

BEATRICE I love you with so much of my heart that none is left to protest. 275

BENEDICK Come, bid me do anything for thee.

BEATRICE Kill Claudio.

BENEDICK Ha? Not for the wide world!

BEATRICE You kill me to deny it. Farewell.

BENEDICK Tarry, sweet Beatrice. 280

He takes her hand

281   *I am gone, though I am here*   my thoughts and feelings are elsewhere even though I am physically still here

288   *Is a' not … villain*   is he not known to be a villain in the highest degree

290   *bear her in hand*   lead her on (i.e. delude her)

291   *uncovered*   naked
unmitigated rancour   sheer malice

292   *in the market-place*   i.e. in the most public place

294   *A proper saying!*   A fine story! (ironic)

298   *counties*   counts
goodly count   (ironic)
count   i.e. Claudio's title; a tale, story; a charge in a legal indictment

299   *Comfect*   candy, sugar-coated

299–300   *for his sake*   i.e. so that I could fight him (Claudio)

301   *curtsies*   courtly (effeminate?) manners
compliment   flattery

302   *turned into tongue*   all talk (and no action)
trim   fine (ironic)

302–3   *He is now … swears it*   these days a man is called courageous who merely brags about his bravery and avows it with a false oath

305   *By this hand*   i.e. his own hand

309   *engaged*   pledged, bound (to challenge Claudio)

310   *By this hand*   i.e. Beatrice's hand

310–11   *render me a dear account*   pay dearly (i.e. with his life) for the debt he owes (i.e. to Hero's honour)

In Act 2 Scene 3 Don Pedro had looked forward eagerly to the first meeting between Beatrice and Benedick when **they hold one an opinion of another's dotage** (lines 169–70). Compare the very different circumstances and mood in which that first meeting takes place.

Claudio accuses Hero of infidelity during the wedding ceremony and Don Pedro and Don John confirm their own eye-witness 'proof'. Hero collapses and when she revives the Friar restores some hope to the distraught Leonato. He proposes that the reported death of Hero will restore Claudio's former feelings for her. Alone for the first time, Beatrice and Benedick awkwardly admit their love and Benedick eventually agrees to avenge the wronged Hero by challenging Claudio.

BEATRICE	I am gone, though I am here. There is no love in you. Nay, I pray you, let me go.	
BENEDICK	Beatrice?	
BEATRICE	In faith, I will go.	
BENEDICK	We'll be friends first.	285
BEATRICE	You dare easier be friends with me than fight with mine enemy?	
BENEDICK	Is Claudio thine enemy?	
BEATRICE	Is 'a not approved in the height a villain that hath slandered, scorned, dishonoured my kinswoman? O that I were a man! What – bear her in hand until they come to take hands? And then with public accusation, uncovered slander, unmitigated rancour – O God, that I were a man! I would eat his heart in the market-place.	290
BENEDICK	Hear me, Beatrice –	
BEATRICE	Talk with a man, out at a window? A proper saying!	
BENEDICK	Nay, but Beatrice –	295
BEATRICE	Sweet Hero! She is wronged, she is slandered, she is undone.	
BENEDICK	Beat –	
BEATRICE	Princes and counties! Surely a princely testimony, a goodly count, Count Comfect: a sweet gallant, surely! O that I were a man for his sake; or that I had any friend would be a man for my sake! But manhood is melted into curtsies, valour into compliment, and men are only turned into tongue – and trim ones, too. He is now as valiant as Hercules that only tells a lie and swears it. I cannot be a man with wishing; therefore I will die a woman with grieving.	300
BENEDICK	Tarry, good Beatrice. By this hand, I love thee.	305
BEATRICE	Use it for my love some other way than swearing by it.	
BENEDICK	Think you, in your soul, the Count Claudio hath wronged Hero?	
BEATRICE	Yea, as sure as I have a thought or a soul.	
BENEDICK	Enough; I am engaged. I will challenge him. I will kiss your hand, and so I leave you. By this hand, Claudio shall render me a dear account. As you hear of me, so think of me. Go comfort your cousin; I must say she is dead; and so farewell.	310

[Exeunt, separately

4:2

The taking of evidence from Borachio and Conrade is obstructed by Dogberry's incompetent cross-examination. The sexton sends for the Watch who confirm that they heard Borachio confess his crime and the Sexton reveals the death of Hero and the flight of Don John.

This short scene is set in a gaol (see Act 3 Scene 5 line 45). How would you arrange the stage to suggest the location and function of the scene?

- *Look at the text for clues about furniture and properties – make a list of the items mentioned.*
- *Can you think of others that would be appropriate: desk, table, charge book, legal documents?*
- *How could stage lighting contribute to create atmosphere?*
- *Would costuming help? Look at the stage directions; the prisoners – clothes torn, dirty?*

1   *dissembly* (for *assembly*)
2   *Sexton* a minor church officer. His duties also included bell ringing and grave digging.
4   *that am I* Dogberry has misunderstood *malefactors* = wrongdoers, criminals
5   *exhibition* (for *commission*). The 'commission' was probably the authority they received from Leonato to *Take their examination yourself* (Act 3 Scene 5 line 38).

'… and write "God" first …'.

16   *defend but* forbid that.   *before* (for *after*)
17–18 *go near to be thought so shortly* everyone will think so soon
19   *none* not (i.e. *false knaves*)
21   *I will go about with him* get the better of, outmanoeuvre (*to go about* is a sailing expression).
       sirrah a common form of address to inferiors
24   *'Fore* before. *they are both in a tale* they both tell the same story
28   *eftest* most convenient (for *aptest*)
29   *accuse* state your charges against
32   *flat perjury* a complete lie

4:2   *Enter* **Dogberry**, **Verges** *and the* **Sexton** (*in gowns*), *the* **watch**,
Conrade *and* **Borachio**

Dogberry	Is our whole dissembly appeared?
Verges	O, a stool and a cushion for the Sexton.
Sexton	Which be the malefactors?
Dogberry	Marry, that am I, and my partner.
Verges	Nay, that's certain; we have the exhibition to examine.

Sexton   But which are the offenders that are to be examined? Let them
come before Master Constable.

Dogberry   Yea, marry, let them come before me. What is your name, friend?

Borachio   Borachio.

Dogberry   Pray write down, 'Borachio'. Yours, sirrah?

Conrade   I am a gentleman, sir, and my name is Conrade.

Dogberry   Write down, 'Master Gentleman Conrade'. Masters, do you serve
God?

Conrade *and*   } Yea, sir, we hope.
Borachio

Dogberry   Write down that they hope they serve God. And write 'God' first,
for God defend but God should go before such villains! Masters, it is
proved already that you are little better than false knaves, and it will go
near to be thought so shortly. How answer you for yourselves?

Conrade   Marry, sir, we say we are none.

Dogberry   [*Aside, to* **Verges** *and the* **Sexton**] A marvellous witty fellow, I assure
you, but I will go about with him. [*Aloud*] Come you hither, sirrah; a
word in your ear, sir. I say to you, it is thought you are false knaves.

Borachio   Sir, I say to you, we are none.

Dogberry   Well, stand aside. 'Fore God, they are both in a tale. Have you writ
down that they are none?

Sexton   Master Constable, you go not the way to examine; you must call
forth the watch that are their accusers.

Dogberry   Yea, marry, that's the eftest way. Let the watch come forth.
Masters, I charge you, in the Prince's name, accuse these men.

First Watch   This man said, sir, that Don John the Prince's brother, was a
villain.

Dogberry   Write down, 'Prince John a villain'. Why, this is flat perjury, to call
a Prince's brother villain.

Borachio   Master Constable –

Dogberry   Pray thee, fellow, peace. I do not like thy look, I promise thee.

Sexton   What heard you him say else?

Line numbers: 5, 10, 15, 20, 25, 30, 35

39 *burglary* (for *perjury*)

40 *by mass* by the mass (a mild oath)

42 *upon his words* on the basis of his (Borachio's) evidence

44 *redemption* (for *damnation*)

51 *bound* bound over (in the legal sense). Dogberry thinks the Sexton means literally.

53 *opinioned* (for *pinioned* = held by the arms)

55 *coxcomb* fool. Professional fools wore a cap shaped like a cockerel's comb.

57 *naughty* wicked

59 *suspect* (for *respect*)

62 *piety* (for *impiety* = irreverence)

66 *go to* i.e. I'll have you know

68 *writ down* recorded (i.e. by the Sexton)

Can you see any similarities between the role of the Friar in the previous scene (Act 4 Scene 1) and that of the Sexton in this scene? Do they represent different forms of authority? How does each seek to bring order out of confusion?

Dogberry's inept interrogation of Borachio and Conrade results in confusion. The Sexton takes charge of the proceedings and quickly exposes the truth of Don John's plot. He leaves to inform Leonato while Dogberry nurses his injured dignity.

SECOND WATCH Marry, that he had received a thousand ducats of Don John for
    accusing the Lady Hero wrongfully.

DOGBERRY Flat burglary as ever was committed.

VERGES Yea, by mass, that it is.   **40**

SEXTON What else, fellow?

FIRST WATCH And that Count Claudio did mean, upon his words, to disgrace
    Hero before the whole assembly, and not marry her.

DOGBERRY O villain – thou wilt be condemned into everlasting redemption
    for this!   **45**

SEXTON What else?

SECOND WATCH This is all.

SEXTON And this is more, masters, than you can deny. Prince John is
    this morning secretly stolen away; Hero was in this manner accused, in
    this very manner refused, and upon the grief of this suddenly died.   **50**
    Master Constable, let these men be bound and brought to Leonato's.
    I will go before and show him their examination.

                                        [Exit

DOGBERRY Come, let them be opinioned.

VERGES Let them be – in the hands.

CONRADE Off, coxcomb!   **55**

DOGBERRY God's my life, where's the Sexton? Let him write down the
    Prince's officer 'coxcomb'. Come, bind them. Thou naughty varlet!

CONRADE Away – you are an ass, you are an ass!

DOGBERRY Dost thou not suspect my place? Dost thou not suspect my
    years? O that he were here, to write me down 'an ass'! But masters,   **60**
    remember that I am 'an ass', though it be not written down, yet forget
    not that I am 'an ass'. No, thou villain, thou art full of piety, as shall be
    proved upon thee by good witness. I am a wise fellow; and, which is
    more, an officer; and, which is more, a householder; and, which is more,
    as pretty a piece of flesh as any is in Messina; and one that knows the   **65**
    law, go to; and a rich fellow enough, go to; and a fellow that hath had
    losses; and one that hath two gowns, and everything handsome about
    him. Bring him away. O that I had been writ down 'an ass'!

                                          [Exeunt

5:1

The anguish of Leonato and Antonio now turns to thoughts of revenge but Claudio and Don Pedro are dismissive of the old men's challenges. Benedick's arrival prompts attempts at light-hearted mockery from his former comrades who are shocked when he challenges Claudio and reveals that Don John has fled. Borachio, under guard, confesses the truth of Don John's plot and Leonato reveals a plan to enable Claudio to atone for the 'death' of Hero.

2	*to second* reinforce (a musical metaphor when one instrument or voice 'answers' another)
3	*counsel* advice
7	*suit with mine* match my own
8	*that so loved* who loved (his child) in the same way
11	*Measure his woe* compare his sorrow with
12	*answer every strain for strain* match in every detail (*strain* means 'tune'). This musical metaphor 'matches' the one from Antonio (i.e. *second*) on line 2.
14	*lineament* characteristic
15	*will smile, and stroke his beard* i.e. often seen as accompanying the home-spun platitudes of the elderly
16	*Bid sorrow, wag* send grief packing *cry 'hem!'* i.e. clear the throat – another preliminary to delivering a lecture of wise platitudes
17	*Patch grief with proverbs* patch over grief's wounds with moral maxims
17–18	*make misfortune … candle-wasters* drown sorrows with philosophy (proverbially scholars and philosophers burnt the night-time candle)
18	*yet* even so
19	*of* from
22	*tasting it* having experienced it
24	*Would give preceptial medicine to rage* would offer wise sayings as cures for emotional anguish
25	*Fetter … silken thread* restrain violent passion with weak words
26	*Charm ache* charm away suffering
27	*'tis all men's office* everyone feels obliged
28	*wring* writhe
29	*sufficiency* capability
30	*To be so moral* i.e. to take his own advice
32	*advertisement* good advice, admonitions
37–8	*However … sufferance* however much they have written with god-like self-confidence and expressed contempt for the sufferings dealt by fate
39	*Yet bend not … yourself* even so, do not take all the suffering on yourself
42	*belied* slandered

5:1   *Enter* LEONATO *and* ANTONIO

ANTONIO   If you go on thus, you will kill yourself,
            And 'tis not wisdom thus to second grief
            Against yourself.
LEONATO   I pray thee cease thy counsel,
            Which falls into mine ears as profitless
            As water in a sieve. Give not me counsel,   5
            Nor let no comforter delight mine ear
            But such a one whose wrongs do suit with mine.
            Bring me a father that so loved his child,
            Whose joy of her is overwhelmed like mine,
            And bid him speak of patience.   10
            Measure his woe the length and breadth of mine,
            And let it answer every strain for strain,
            As thus for thus, and such a grief for such,
            In every lineament, branch, shape and form.
            If such a one will smile, and stroke his beard,   15
            Bid sorrow, wag, cry 'hem' when he should groan,
            Patch grief with proverbs, make misfortune drunk
            With candle-wasters – bring him yet to me
            And I of him will gather patience.
            But there is no such man; for brother, men   20
            Can counsel and speak comfort to that grief
            Which they themselves not feel; but tasting it,
            Their counsel turns to passion, which before
            Would give preceptial medicine to rage,
            Fetter strong madness in a silken thread,   25
            Charm ache with air and agony with words.
            No, no; 'tis all men's office to speak patience
            To those that wring under the load of sorrow,
            But no man's virtue nor sufficiency
            To be so moral when he shall endure   30
            The like himself. Therefore give me no counsel;
            My griefs cry louder than advertisement.
ANTONIO   Therein do men from children nothing differ.
LEONATO   I pray thee, peace. I will be flesh and blood,
            For there was never yet philosopher   35
            That could endure the toothache patiently,
            However they have writ the style of gods
            And made a push at chance and sufferance.
ANTONIO   Yet bend not all the harm upon yourself;
            Make those that do offend you suffer too.   40
LEONATO   There thou speak'st reason. Nay, I will do so.
            My soul doth tell me Hero is belied;

111

45 *hastily* in haste

46 *Good den* short for 'God give you good even(ing)'

49 *Are you so hasty now?* Leonato recalls that Don Pedro had originally been in no hurry to leave (see Act 1 Scene 1 line 110).
all is one it doesn't matter now

53 *thou dissembler* you hypocrite. Leonato now refers to Claudio in the second person singular form of *thou/thee* as a mark of his contempt. Claudio still uses the respectful 'you' form.

55 *beshrew* curse

58 *Tush, tush* a dismissively contemptuous exclamation
fleer sneer

*Leonato rebukes Claudio for insolently choosing to **fleer and jest** at him (line 58).*

* *Allocate parts and read aloud lines 45–58. Use the information in the stage directions and any clues in the text. Is Leonato right to be offended – or is he over-reacting?*
* *What is the tone of Claudio's and Don Pedro's remarks in this episode: patronising, dignified, contemptuous, respectful, insulting, mocking, dismissive, cruel, indifferent, amused?*
* *Do Claudio and Don Pedro respond differently at all?*
* *How do Leonato and Antonio behave in this exchange: are they ridiculous figures – or do they prompt your compassion?*

59 *dotard* senile old man

60 *As under privilege of age to brag* using my age as a shield for boasting (i.e. knowing that as an old man he cannot be challenged)

62 *to thy head* to your face

64 *lay my reverence by* set aside my age and the respect it merits

65 *bruise of many days* a lifetime's blows

66 *trial of a man* trial by combat

70 *where never scandal slept* i.e. none of his ancestors buried in the family tomb were tainted with disgrace

71 *framed* formed, shaped

75 *nice fence* skilful sword-play

76 *May of youth* The springtime month of May was traditionally associated with the vigour and energy of youth.
lustihood physical fitness

And that shall Claudio know, so shall the Prince,
And all of them that thus dishonour her.

Enter **Don Pedro** *and* **Claudio**

Antonio	Here comes the Prince and Claudio hastily.	45

Don Pedro Good den, good den.

Claudio Good day to both of you.

Leonato Hear you, my lords –

Don Pedro We have some haste, Leonato.

They do not stop

Leonato Some haste, my lord? Well, fare you well, my lord.
Are you so hasty now? Well, all is one.

Don Pedro [*Returning*] Nay, do not quarrel with us, good old man. 50

Antonio If he could right himself with quarrelling
Some of us would lie low.

Claudio Who wrongs him?

Leonato Marry, thou dost wrong me, thou dissembler, thou!
Nay, never lay hand upon thy sword;
I fear thee not.

Claudio Marry, beshrew my hand 55
If it should give your age such cause of fear.
In faith, my hand meant nothing to my sword.

Leonato Tush, tush, man, never fleer and jest at me.
I speak not like a dotard nor a fool,
As under privilege of age to brag 60
What I have done being young, or what would do
Were I not old. Know, Claudio, to thy head,
Thou hast so wronged mine innocent child and me
That I am forced to lay my reverence by,
And with grey hairs and bruise of many days, 65
Do challenge thee to trial of a man.
I say thou hast belied mine innocent child.
Thy slander hath gone through and through her heart,
And she lies buried with her ancestors –
O, in a tomb where never scandal slept, 70
Save this of hers, framed by thy villainy!

Claudio My villainy?

Leonato Thine, Claudio, thine, I say.

Don Pedro You say not right, old man.

Leonato My lord, my lord,
I'll prove it on his body if he dare,
Despite his nice fence and his active practice, 75
His May of youth and bloom of lustihood.

78   *daff* i.e. *doff* = brush aside

82   *Win me and wear me* beat me first and only then will I submit to you

83   *boy* used contemptuously to suggest that Claudio is not a real man

84   *I'll whip you from your foining fence* Antonio contrasts real fighting with the thrust and parry of fencing strokes (*foining* = thrusting)

89   *answer a man indeed* respond to the challenge of a real man

91   *apes, braggarts, Jacks, milk-sops* imitators (of men), boasters, knaves, feeble boys

93   *what they weigh* what they are worth
     scruple smallest amount

94   *Scambling, outfacing, fashion-mongering* brawling, swaggering, fashion-following (i.e. shallow, superficial)

95   *cog and flout, deprave* cheat (as in a sleight of hand with dice or cards) and mock, defame

96   *Go anticly* behave like buffoons
     show outward hideousness put on the mask (i.e. appearance) of grotesque fierceness

98   *if they durst* if they chose

102 *wake your patience* disturb you any longer

105 *very full of proof* fully proved

113 *fray* fight

Leonato restrains his incensed brother.

CLAUDIO	Away; I will not have to do with you.
LEONATO	Canst thou so daff me? Thou hast killed my child;
	If thou kill'st me, boy, thou shalt kill a man.
ANTONIO	He shall kill two of us and men indeed.

He shall kill two of us and men indeed.   80
But that's no matter; let him kill one first.
Win me and wear me, let him answer me.
Come, follow me, boy, come, sir boy, come follow me
Sir boy, I'll whip you from your foining fence;
Nay, as I am a gentleman, I will.   85

LEONATO   Brother –

ANTONIO   Content yourself. God knows, I loved my niece;
And she is dead, slandered to death by villains,
That dare as well answer a man indeed
As I dare take a serpent by the tongue.   90
Boys, apes, braggarts, Jacks, milk-sops!

LEONATO   Brother Antony –

ANTONIO   Hold you content. What, man! I know them, yea,
And what they weigh, even to the utmost scruple –
Scambling, outfacing, fashion-mongering boys,
That lie and cog and flout, deprave and slander,   95
Go anticly and show outward hideousness,
And speak off half a dozen dangerous words
How they might hurt their enemies, if they durst;
And this is all.

LEONATO   But, brother Antony –

ANTONIO   Come, 'tis no matter   100
Do not you meddle, let me deal in this.

DON PEDRO Gentlemen both, we will not wake your patience;
My heart is sorry for your daughter's death,
But on my honour she was charged with nothing
But what was true, and very full of proof.   105

LEONATO   My lord, my lord –

DON PEDRO I will not hear you.

LEONATO   No? Come, brother, away; I will be heard.

ANTONIO   And shall, or some of us will smart for it.

[Exeunt **LEONATO** *and* **ANTONIO**

Enter **BENEDICK**

DON PEDRO See, see, here comes the man we went to seek.   110

CLAUDIO   Now, signor, what news?

BENEDICK   Good day, my lord.

DON PEDRO Welcome, signor; you are almost come to part almost a fray.

114 *had like to have* were about to have. *with* by

117 *doubt* suspect

119 *up and down to seek thee* looking everywhere for you

119–20 *high-proof melancholy* extremely depressed

120 *and would fain* and would very much like to

121 *It is in my scabbard* i.e. Benedick is in the mood for fighting rather than humour, though Don Pedro and Claudio assume he is just being witty.

123 *Never any* no one ever. *beside their wit* i.e. mad

124 *draw* Claudio puns on taking a sword from its scabbard and a musical instrument from its case.

126 *though care killed a cat* a proverbial saying

127 *mettle* spirit, courage

128 *in the career* at full charge (from jousting)
charge level it; urge it on (like a horse at full gallop)

130 *staff* lance
broke cross a lance that was snapped across the body of the opponent was regarded as poor tilting. A direct hit on the opponent would result in the lance splintering. Claudio implies that Benedick's first 'charge' of wit was not up to standard and calls for another bout.

131–2 *angry indeed* really angry (as opposed to pretending)

133 *turn his girdle* a common expression used here light-heartedly by Claudio. It may refer to wresting in which the buckle of the belt was turned to the back as a preparation for a contest.

134 *in your ear* i.e. privately

135 *bless* keep, save

136 *make it good* prove it

137 *with what* i.e. with whatever weapons
Do me right give me satisfaction

138 *protest* state publicly

139 *hear from you* i.e. receive your formal response to my challenge

140 *cheer* entertainment

142–4 *calf's head … capon … woodcock* All three dishes in Claudio's fanciful 'feast' are synonymous with foolishness.

143 *curiously* skilfully.
naught useless. Claudio's use of *carve* and *knife* may also pun on the sword and duelling strokes.

145 *ambles well* i.e. like a slow-plodding horse, suitable for a lady

147 *fine* delicate, refined

148 *gross* bloated, over-indulged

149 *Just* exactly

150 *wise gentleman* ironic (i.e. a fool)

150–1 *hath the tongues* speaks foreign languages

154 *trans-shape* transform, distort

155 *properest* most handsome

CLAUDIO   We had like to have had our two noses snapped off with two old
      men without teeth –   115

DON PEDRO Leonato and his brother. What think'st thou? Had we fought, I
      doubt we should have been too young for them.

BENEDICK   In a false quarrel there is no true valour. I come to seek you both.

CLAUDIO   We have been up and down to seek thee, for we are high-proof
      melancholy and would fain have it beaten away. Wilt thou use thy wit?   120

BENEDICK   It is in my scabbard – shall I draw it?

DON PEDRO Dost thou wear thy wit by thy side?

CLAUDIO   Never any did so, though very many have been beside their wit. I
      will bid thee draw, as we do the minstrels: draw to pleasure us.

DON PEDRO As I am an honest man, he looks pale. Art thou sick, or angry?   125

CLAUDIO   What? Courage, man. What though care killed a cat; thou hast
      mettle enough in thee to kill care.

BENEDICK   Sir, I shall meet your wit in the career, an you charge it against me.
      I pray you, choose another subject.

CLAUDIO   Nay then, give him another staff; this last was broke cross.   130

DON PEDRO By this light, he changes more and more. I think he be angry
      indeed.

CLAUDIO   If he be, he knows how to turn his girdle.

BENEDICK   Shall I speak a word in your ear?

CLAUDIO   God bless me from a challenge!   135

BENEDICK [*Aside to* CLAUDIO] You are a villain; I jest not. I will make it good how
      you dare, with what you dare, and when you dare. Do me right, or I will
      protest your cowardice. You have killed a sweet lady, and her death
      shall fall heavy on you. Let me hear from you.

CLAUDIO   Well, I will meet you, so I may have good cheer.   140

DON PEDRO What, a feast, a feast?

CLAUDIO   I'faith I thank him. He hath bid me to a calf's head and capon, the
      which, if I do not carve most curiously, say my knife's naught. Shall I
      not find a woodcock too?

BENEDICK   Sir, your wit ambles well; it goes easily.   145

DON PEDRO I'll tell thee how Beatrice praised thy wit the other day. I said thou
      hadst a fine wit. 'True,' said she, 'a fine little one.' 'No,' said I, 'a great
      wit.' 'Right,' says she, 'a great gross one.' 'Nay,' said I, 'a good wit.'
      'Just,' said she, 'it hurts nobody!' 'Nay,' said I, 'the gentleman is wise.'
      'Certain,' said she, 'a wise gentleman.' 'Nay,' said I, 'he hath the   150
      tongues.' 'That I believe,' said she, 'for he swore a thing to me on
      Monday night, which he forswore on Tuesday morning – there's a
      double tongue, there's two tongues.' Thus did she, an hour together,
      trans-shape thy particular virtues; yet at last she concluded with a sigh,
      thou wast the properest man in Italy.   155

158 *the old man's daughter* i.e. Hero

159 *God saw him … garden* A reference to the biblical story of Adam and Eve and the Garden of Eden. They tried to hide themselves from God among the trees when they had disobeyed Him by eating the apple of the Tree of Knowledge (Genesis Chapter 3).

160–2 *But when … married man'* Don Pedro and Claudio remind Benedick of his boast at Act 1 Scene 1 lines 194–5.

164 *gossip-like humour* frivolous tittle-tattle
as braggarts do their blades i.e. like boasting cowards who break their swords and pretend it happened in fight

168 *Lord Lackbeard* i.e. Claudio. Benedick suggests he lacks masculine qualities.
I shall meet i.e. for the duel

Look in detail at Benedick's last speech in the scene (lines 163–9).
How would you direct it in order finally to convince Don Pedro and
Claudio that **He is in earnest** (line 170)?

- *Does Benedick pause before delivering the speech; laugh ironically before becoming instantly serious; turn away and then back; place his hand on his sword?*
- *Which words and phrases carry particular impact: **boy**, **braggarts**, **Lord Lackbeard** … ? How would they be delivered? What is their effect?*
- *How is the speech delivered: emotionally, coldly, with grim courtesy, with dignified restraint, with barely contained fury, with quiet menace?*
- *How does Benedick address Don Pedro: with a salute, as his superior officer; with a formal handshake, as a former friend; with a stiff formal bow?*
- *How do Claudio and Don Pedro react during the speech: exchange troubled glances; laughter fading to grim seriousness; stony-faced – and when he leaves?*

Try out a number of different versions. Which work best?

---

175 *pretty* fine (ironic)

175–6 *when he … off his wit* i.e. discards his cloak (of intelligence) in readiness for a fight

177–8 *He is then … such a man* a man who challenges another (i.e. like Benedick) may seem like a hero to a fool (*ape*), whereas the fool is the wiser of the two

179 *soft you, let me be* hang on, let me think
pluck up … sad pull yourself together and be serious (addressed to himself)

181–2 *she shall … balance* Perhaps Dogberry confuses the traditional image of the scales of justice with household or commercial scales with an unconscious pun on *reasons*/'raisins'.

182 *an* if

185 *Hearken after* enquire about

188 *secondarily* (for secondly). *slanders* (for slanderers)

189 *belied* misrepresented

194 *in his own division* using his own brand of logic

195 *well-suited* well-dressed (i.e. saying the same thing in several different ways)

CLAUDIO   For the which she wept heartily, and said she cared not.

DON PEDRO Yea, that she did. But yet for all that, an if she did not hate him
      deadly, she would love him dearly; the old man's daughter told us all.

CLAUDIO   All, all; and moreover, God saw him when he was hid in the garden.

DON PEDRO But when shall we set the savage bull's horns on the sensible   **160**
      Benedick's head?

CLAUDIO   Yea, and text underneath, 'Here dwells Benedick, the married man'?

BENEDICK   Fare you well, boy; you know my mind. I will leave you now to your
      gossip-like humour. You break jests as braggarts do their blades –
      which God be thanked hurt not. [*To* **DON PEDRO**] My lord, for your many   **165**
      courtesies I thank you; I must discontinue your company. Your brother
      the Bastard is fled from Messina. You have among you killed a sweet
      and innocent lady. For my Lord Lackbeard there, he and I shall meet;
      and till then, peace be with him.

                                                                  [*Exit*

DON PEDRO He is in earnest.   **170**

CLAUDIO   In most profound earnest, and I'll warrant you, for the love of
      Beatrice.

DON PEDRO And hath challenged thee?

CLAUDIO   Most sincerely.

DON PEDRO What a pretty thing man is, when he goes in his doublet and hose   **175**
      and leaves off his wit!

CLAUDIO   He is then a giant to an ape; but then is an ape a doctor to such a
      man.

DON PEDRO But soft you, let me be; pluck up, my heart, and be sad. Did he not
      say my brother was fled?   **180**

     Enter **DOGBERRY**, **VERGES**, **CONRADE** *and* **BORACHIO** *with the* **WATCH**

DOGBERRY   Come you, sir. If justice cannot tame you, she shall ne'er weigh
      more reasons in her balance. Nay, an you be a cursing hypocrite once,
      you must be looked to.

DON PEDRO How now? Two of my brother's men bound – Borachio one?

CLAUDIO   Hearken after their offence, my lord.   **185**

DON PEDRO Officers, what offence have these men done?

DOGBERRY   Marry, sir, they have committed false report; moreover, they have
      spoken untruths; secondarily, they are slanders; sixth and lastly, they
      have belied a lady; thirdly, they have verified unjust things; and, to
      conclude, they are lying knaves.   **190**

DON PEDRO First, I ask thee what they have done; thirdly, I ask thee, what's
      their offence; sixth and lastly, why they are committed; and, to
      conclude, what you lay to their charge?

CLAUDIO   Rightly reasoned, and in his own division; and by my troth there's
      one meaning well-suited.   **195**

196–7 *bound to your answer* i.e. physically *bound* with ropes and legally *bound* (summoned) to answer the charges

197 *cunning* clever

199 *go no farther to mine answer* go no further without answering your question (and being punished)

203 *incensed* instigated

205 *should marry* should have married

206 *seal* bring to a close

212 *set thee on* incite you

217 *rare semblance* lovely appearance

218 *plaintiffs* (for *defendants*)

219 *reformed* (for *informed*)

220 *shall serve* present an opportunity

226 *slave* wretch

233 *if you bethink you of it* if you think about it (the whole speech is heavily sarcastic)

234 *pray* implore

DON PEDRO Who have you offended, masters, that you are thus bound to your answer? This learned Constable is too cunning to be understood. What's your offence?

BORACHIO Sweet Prince, let me go no farther to mine answer. Do you hear me and let this Count kill me. I have deceived even your very eyes. What   200 your wisdoms could not discover, these shallow fools have brought to light; who in the night overheard me confessing to this man, how Don John, your brother, incensed me to slander the Lady Hero; how you were brought into the orchard and saw me court Margaret in Hero's garments; how you disgraced her when you should marry her. My   205 villainy they have upon record, which I had rather seal with my death than repeat over to my shame. The lady is dead upon mine and my master's false accusation. And briefly, I desire nothing but the reward of a villain.

DON PEDRO Runs not this speech like iron through your blood?   210

CLAUDIO I have drunk poison whiles he uttered it.

DON PEDRO But did my brother set thee on to this?

BORACHIO Yea, and paid me richly for the practice of it.

DON PEDRO He is composed and framed of treachery.
And fled he is upon this villainy.   215

CLAUDIO Sweet Hero, now thy image doth appear
In the rare semblance that I loved it first.

DOGBERRY Come, bring away the plaintiffs; by this time our Sexton hath reformed Signor Leonato of the matter. And masters, do not forget to specify, when time and place shall serve, that I am an ass.   220

VERGES Here, here comes master Signor Leonato, and the Sexton too.

Enter **LEONATO**, **ANTONIO** *and the* **SEXTON**

LEONATO Which is the villain? Let me see his eyes
That when I note another man like him
I may avoid him. Which of these is he?

BORACHIO If you would know your wronger, look on me.   225

LEONATO Art thou the slave that with thy breath hast killed
Mine innocent child?

BORACHIO   Yea, even I alone.

LEONATO No, not so, villain, thou beliest thyself.
Here stand a pair of honourable men,
A third is fled, that had a hand in it.   230
I thank you, Princes, for my daughter's death,
Record it with your high and worthy deeds.
'Twas bravely done, if you bethink you of it.

CLAUDIO I know not how to pray your patience,
Yet I must speak. Choose your revenge yourself;   235

236   *Impose me to* impose on me
          invention ingenuity

Don Pedro refers to Leonato as **this good old man** (line 239). His respect and submission are in sharp contrast to his and Claudio's attitude earlier in the scene. Make a note of earlier examples of their scorn or mockery.

---

241   *That he'll enjoin me to* that he will require of me

244   *Possess* inform

245–6 *if your love … invention* if your feelings for her can create anything in the way of elegy

254   *Give her the right* i.e. make her your wife

257–8 *and dispose/For henceforth of poor Claudio* i.e. and place my life at your disposal

259   *expect* await

260   *naughty* wicked (a much stronger condemnation than today's meaning)

262   *packed* an accomplice

266   *by her* about her

267   *under white and black* in black and white (i.e. in writing)

270   *one Deformed* another misunderstanding of Borachio's talk of fashion being a *deformed thief* (Act 3 Scene 3 line 94). The Second Watch had thought he was referring to a thief called Deformed!
          key … lock The lovelock of Act 3 Scene 3 line 126 has transformed itself in Dogberry's imagination.

271   *in God's name* claiming to be for a religious purpose; it was common for those asking for charity to quote from the Bible that 'He that hath pity on the poor, lendeth to the Lord' (Proverbs Chapter 19 verse 17)

Impose me to what penance your invention
Can lay upon my sin; yet sinned I not
But in mistaking.

DON PEDRO   By my soul, nor I.
And yet, to satisfy this good old man,
I would bend under any heavy weight   240
That he'll enjoin me to.

LEONATO   I cannot bid you bid my daughter live,
That were impossible. But I pray you both,
Possess the people in Messina here
How innocent she died; and if your love   245
Can labour aught in sad invention,
Hang her an epitaph upon her tomb
And sing it to her bones, sing it tonight.
Tomorrow morning, come you to my house;
And since you could not be my son-in-law,   250
Be yet my nephew. My brother hath a daughter
Almost the copy of my child that's dead,
And she alone is heir to both of us.
Give her the right you should have giv'n her cousin,
And so dies my revenge.

CLAUDIO   O noble sir,   255
Your over-kindness doth wring tears from me.
I do embrace your offer, and dispose
For henceforth of poor Claudio.

LEONATO   Tomorrow then, I will expect your coming;
Tonight I take my leave. This naughty man   260
Shall face to face be brought to Margaret,
Who I believe was packed in all this wrong,
Hired to it by your brother.

BORACHIO   No, by my soul, she was not;
Nor knew not what she did when she spoke to me,
But always hath been just and virtuous   265
In anything that I do know by her.

DOGBERRY   Moreover, sir, which indeed is not under white and black, this
plaintiff here, the offender, did call me ass. I beseech you, let it be
remembered in his punishment. And also, the watch heard them talk of
one Deformed – they say he wears a key in his ear and a lock hanging by   270
it, and borrows money in God's name, the which he hath used so long
and never paid, that now men grow hard-hearted and will lend nothing
for God's sake. Pray you, examine him upon that point.

LEONATO   I thank thee for thy care and honest pains.

DOGBERRY   Your worship speaks like a most thankful and reverend youth, and I   275
praise God for you.

LEONATO   There's for thy pains. [*He gives him money*]

123

278   *God save the foundation!*   an expression used by those receiving charity at the gates of religious houses

281   *to correct yourself*   Dogberry is confused. It is the criminals who will be (punished)

283   *give*   (for *ask*)

284   *prohibit*   (for *permit*)

The final departure of Dogberry (lines 274–84) can bring a welcome comic release from the tensions of this long and varied scene.

Leonato finds it difficult get rid of him:

- Does Dogberry realise that Leonato is expecting him to go?
- How does Dogberry react to Leonato's tip: with exaggerated gratitude; shaking/kissing his hand; pocketing it from Verges?
- Could Leonato give him something else at line 277: medal, gold chain?
- Could Leonato keep trying to exit during lines 280–4?

287   *with Hero*   i.e. at her tomb

289   *lewd*   base

Leonato and Antonio are incensed but powerless. Claudio and Don Pedro welcome Benedick's arrival and attempt facetious banter but gradually realise the deadly nature of his challenge. Their unease turns to remorse as Borachio reveals his part in disgracing Hero. Leonato reveals a plan for Claudio to atone.

5:2

Benedick exchanges sexual banter with Margaret's in requesting her help in meeting Beatrice. When she arrives the serious business of his challenge to Claudio combines with embarrassed verbal sparring. Ursula brings news of the discovery of Don John's plot.

At this stage the characters know nothing of the revealed truth of Don John's plot. How does Margaret react here: subdued, shameless, embarrassed? In one production Margaret entered carrying a suitcase, intending to sneak away – but thought better of it. Do you have any other ideas?

1   *deserve well at my hands*   earn my gratitude (i.e. she will be rewarded)

4   *so high a style*   such an ornate style (with a pun on 'stile')
       come over it   better it; climb over it

5   *comely*   fitting, appropriate; good-looking

6   *come over me*   i.e. in a sexual sense

6–7   *keep below stairs*   remain as a servant (i.e. never become a 'mistress')

8   *it catches*   it bites

9   *fencer's foils*   light swords made blunt for fencing practice

11   *bucklers*   shields, i.e. Benedick concedes victory to Margaret in this battle of wit

12   *Give us the swords … our own*   Margaret continues the sexual banter. Here *swords* and *bucklers* are associated with the sexual organs, penis and vagina.

DOGBERRY	God save the foundation!
LEONATO	Go, I discharge thee of thy prisoner, and I thank thee.
DOGBERRY	I leave an arrant knave with your worship, which I beseech your 280 worship to correct yourself for the example of others. God keep your worship, I wish your worship well. God restore you to health; I humbly give you leave to depart, and if a merry meeting may be wished, God prohibit it! Come, neighbour.

[Exeunt **DOGBERRY** *and* **VERGES**

LEONATO	Until tomorrow morning, lords, farewell.	285
ANTONIO	Farewell, my lords; we look for you tomorrow.	
DON PEDRO	We will not fail.	
CLAUDIO	Tonight I'll mourn with Hero.	

[Exeunt **DON PEDRO** *and* **CLAUDIO**

LEONATO	Bring you these fellows on. We'll talk with Margaret, How her acquaintance grew with this lewd fellow.

[Exeunt

5:2	*Enter* **BENEDICK** *and* **MARGARET**

BENEDICK	Pray thee, sweet Mistress Margaret, deserve well at my hands by helping me to the speech of Beatrice.	
MARGARET	Will you then write me a sonnet in praise of my beauty?	
BENEDICK	In so high a style, Margaret, that no man living shall come over it, for in most comely truth thou deservest it.	5
MARGARET	To have no man come over me! Why, shall I always keep below stairs?	
BENEDICK	Thy wit is as quick as the greyhound's mouth; it catches.	
MARGARET	And yours as blunt as the fencer's foils, which hit but hurt not.	
BENEDICK	A most manly wit, Margaret, it will not hurt a woman. And so I pray thee call Beatrice; I give thee the bucklers.	10
MARGARET	Give us the swords; we have bucklers of our own.	

13 *pikes* the central spikes in round shields (again it refers to the penis).
vice screw (the shield spike would be screwed into the shield but it also has an obvious sexual meaning). A *vice* is also a tool made of two jaws tightened by a screw and used by carpenters to clamp a piece of work in position (again there is a sexual allusion to thighs closed in intercourse which in turn leads on to the reference to Beatrice's *legs* (line 15).

14 *maids* virgins

21 *Leander* See the note to Act 4 Scene 1 line 74.

21–2 *Troilus … pandars* In Greek legend, Troilus, a Trojan prince, fell in love with Cressida. When she was exchanged for a Trojan prisoner of war, Cressida swore to be faithful to Troilus, but then deceived him with Diomed. Troilus was killed by Achilles. The word *pandars* comes from Cressida's uncle, Pandarus, who acted as go-between for the two lovers.

22–3 *quondam carpet-mongers* former frequenters of ladies' bedrooms (which were carpeted)

23 *yet* even so

24 *turned over and over* turned head over heels

26 *innocent* silly

27 *'horn' … hard* both refer to sexual erection as well as the familiar cuckold's horns

28 *ominous endings* as rhymes they end the line of verse (*endings*) but are unpromising (*ominous*) in being unlikely to win his lady's favour

29 *in festival terms* in a style suitable for public exhibition

34 *with that I came* with what I came for (i.e. to find out about the challenge)

> *Benedick's … I will kiss thee* (line 36) is the first clear attempt at physical intimacy between the new 'lovers' in the scene.
>
> Several issues complicate their courtship: Hero's disgrace; Benedick's challenge to Claudio; their former **merry war**.
>
> Their awkwardness is often exploited to comic effect on stage. How would you direct the moment?
>
> • The 'kiss': does Benedick try to take Beatrice by surprise; does she dodge away; does she thrust something in front of her face – hat, fan, Benedick's crumpled poem?
> • Is Beatrice flippant, serious, flirtatious, breathless?
> • Do they kiss during the scene: at what point(s) – and who initiates it?
> • Do they kiss tenderly, passionately, awkwardly?
> • How do they react: relieved, turning away, gazing into each other's eyes?

38 *noisome* disgusting, offensive

39 *frighted* distorted, twisted

40 *undergoes my challenge* has been challenged

41 *subscribe* proclaim him publicly (i.e. in writing)

44 *so politic a state of evil* such a well-ordered rule

46 *suffer* allow; put up with

47 *a good epithet* a good description

49 *In spite of your heart* against your inclinations

50 *spite* torment

51 *friend* lover

BENEDICK   If you use them, Margaret, you must put in the pikes with a vice; and they are dangerous weapons for maids.

MARGARET   Well, I will call Beatrice to you, who I think hath legs.   15

[*Exit*

BENEDICK   And therefore will come.

[*Sings*]   The God of Love
That sits above,
And knows me, and knows me,
How pitiful I deserve –   20

I mean in singing. But in loving, Leander the good swimmer, Troilus the first employer of pandars, and a whole bookful of these quondam carpet-mongers, whose names yet run smoothly in the even road of a blank verse – why, they were never so truly turned over and over as my poor self in love. Marry, I cannot show it in rhyme – I have tried: I can   25 find out no rhyme to 'lady' but 'baby' – an innocent rhyme; for 'scorn', 'horn' – a hard rhyme; for 'school', 'fool' – a babbling rhyme, very ominous endings. No, I was not born under a rhyming planet, nor I cannot woo in festival terms.

Enter **BEATRICE**

Sweet Beatrice, wouldst thou come when I called thee.   30

BEATRICE   Yea, Signor, and depart when you bid me.

BENEDICK   O stay but till then.

BEATRICE   'Then' is spoken; fare you well now. And yet, ere I go, let me go with that I came – which is, with knowing what hath passed between you and Claudio.   35

BENEDICK   Only foul words, and thereupon I will kiss thee.

BEATRICE   Foul words is but foul wind, and foul wind is but foul breath, and foul breath is noisome – therefore, I will depart unkissed.

BENEDICK   Thou hast frighted the word out of his right sense, so forcible is thy wit. But I must tell thee plainly: Claudio undergoes my challenge, and   40 either I must shortly hear from him, or I will subscribe him a coward. And I pray thee now tell me, for which of my bad parts didst thou first fall in love with me?

BEATRICE   For them all together, which maintained so politic a state of evil that they will not admit any good part to intermingle with them. But for   45 which of my good parts did you first suffer love for me?

BENEDICK   'Suffer love'? A good epithet: I do suffer love indeed, for I love thee against my will!

BEATRICE   In spite of your heart, I think. Alas, poor heart! If you spite it for my sake, I will spite it for yours, for I will never love that which my   50 friend hates.

BENEDICK   Thou and I are too wise to woo peaceably.

53 *It appears not in the confession* Your claim to wisdom isn't borne out by your statement

55 *instance* saying, example

55–6 *in the time of good neighbours* when good neighbours existed (a reference to the saying, 'He who praises himself has ill neighbours')

56 *in this age* these days.
tomb memorial (i.e. his reputation)

57 *he shall live no longer* his memory won't survive. *bell* i.e. funeral bell

60 *Question* i.e. that's a good question.
clamour noise (of the funeral bell)
rheum weeping (of the widow)

61 *expedient* advisable.
Don Worm i.e. his conscience (a metaphor from the Bible)

62–3 *to be the trumpet … virtues* to blow his own trumpet

63 *So much for* that's enough of

69 *mend* get better, recover

71 *yonder's old coil* there's a great commotion

73 *abused* deceived, taken in

74 *presently* immediately

76 *die* a common metaphor for sexual orgasm
be buried in thy eyes i.e. he will see his own image reflected as he gazes into her eyes

> Compare the way Beatrice and Benedick talk to each other here with their exchanges in Act 1 Scene 1 and Act 2 Scene 1.
>
> Also compare their way of courting with that of Claudio and Hero, particularly in Act 2 Scene 1 lines 223–37.

Benedick seeks Margaret's help in meeting Beatrice and then laments that he has no aptitude for expressing his love in the conventional way. When Beatrice arrives he confirms his challenge to Claudio and they self-consciously talk of love. Ursula brings news of the discovery of Don John's plot.

5:3

Claudio fulfils the first part of his promise to Leonato by reading a tribute to Hero's innocence. Balthasar sings a solemn hymn to the Moon, goddess of virginity, and Claudio promises to commemorate the anniversary of Hero's death.

In Shakespeare's open air theatre the stage direction **with tapers** *indicates a night-time scene. In a modern theatre, lighting effects can help to produce a striking visual spectacle.*

How would you create an impressive ritual? Look for clues to props and movement in the text:

- *setting: chapel, tomb, crypt?*
- *lighting: subdued, candles, lanterns, torches?*
- *attendants: procession, priest, choirboys, monks, religious emblems?*
- *military ceremony: slow march, swords, salutes, wreaths?*
- *music: organ, unaccompanied chanting; Balthasar's song – guitar, lute?*

s.d. *with tapers* carrying candles

1 *monument* family burial chamber

5 *guerdon* reward for

7 *with* from

BEATRICE   It appears not in the confession; there's not one wise man among
            twenty that will praise himself.

BENEDICK   An old, an old instance, Beatrice, that lived in the time of good   55
            neighbours. If a man do not erect in this age his own tomb ere he dies,
            he shall live no longer in monument than the bell rings and the widow
            weeps.

BEATRICE   And how long is that, think you?

BENEDICK   Question – why, an hour in clamour and a quarter in rheum.   60
            Therefore is it most expedient for the wise – if Don Worm, his
            conscience, find no impediment to the contrary – to be the trumpet of
            his own virtues, as I am to myself. So much for praising myself, who I
            myself will bear witness is praise-worthy. And now tell me, how doth
            your cousin?   65

BEATRICE   Very ill.

BENEDICK   And how do you?

BEATRICE   Very ill too.

BENEDICK   Serve God, love me, and mend. There will I leave you too, for here
            comes one in haste.   70

                            Enter URSULA

URSULA   Madam, you must come to your uncle; yonder's old coil at home. It
            is proved my Lady Hero hath been falsely accused, the Prince and
            Claudio mightily abused and Don John is the author of all, who is fled
            and gone. Will you come presently?

BEATRICE   Will you go hear this news, signor?   75

BENEDICK   I will live in thy heart, die in thy lap, and be buried in thy eyes. And
            moreover, I will go with thee to thy uncle's.

                                                                        [*Exeunt*

5:3   *Enter* CLAUDIO, DON PEDRO, BALTHASAR, *and three or
                         four attendant lords, with tapers*

CLAUDIO   Is this the monument to Leonato?

A LORD   It is, my lord.

CLAUDIO   [*Reading from a scroll*]

                            Epitaph
            Done to death by slanderous tongues
                Was the Hero that here lies.
            Death, in guerdon of her wrongs,   5
                Gives her fame which never dies.
            So the life that died with shame
                Lives in death with glorious fame.

12	*goddess of the night* i.e. Diana, goddess of the moon and patroness of virgins
13	*knight* As a virgin, Hero is represented as a devoted servant or follower of Diana.
15	*Round about her tomb* Circling the tomb in a clockwise direction was the traditional way of averting evil.
19–20	*Graves yawn … utterèd* i.e. may nothing be at peace until Hero's death has been properly commemorated
23	*rite* ceremony
25	*have preyed* have finished hunting
26	*Before* in front of *the wheels of Phoebus* Apollo, the sun god, was represented as driving his chariot across the sky to bring the daylight.
29	*several* separate
30	*weeds* clothes (i.e. for the wedding)
32	*Hymen* god of marriage *issue* outcome *speed's* bring us
33	*for whom* i.e. Hero

Night turns to day as the scene draws to a close; the time has come to look to the future. Compare the ceremony of mourning and commemoration in this scene with the formalities of the unmasking ceremony in the next (Act 5 Scene 4). Is Claudio a changed man?

In a solemn ceremony Claudio pays tribute to Hero's innocence and a hymn is sung in her praise. This brings a measure of closure to Hero's tragedy and thoughts turn to the marriage which will bring final reconciliation.

Hang thou there upon the tomb
  Praising her when I am dumb.   **10**
[*He hangs the scroll on the tomb*]

Now music sound, and sing your solemn hymn.

BALTHASAR [*Sings*]
Pardon, goddess of the night,
Those that slew thy virgin knight,
For the which with songs of woe
Round about her tomb they go.   **15**
Midnight assist our moan,
Help us to sigh and groan,
  Heavily, heavily.
Graves yawn and yield your dead,
Till death be utterèd,   **20**
  Heavily, heavily.

CLAUDIO   Now unto thy bones, good night;
Yearly will I do this rite.

DON PEDRO Good morrow, masters; put your torches out,
The wolves have preyed, and look, the gentle day   **25**
Before the wheels of Phoebus, round about
Dapples the drowsy east with spots of grey.
Thanks to you all, and leave us. Fare you well.

CLAUDIO   Good morrow masters, each his several way.

[*Exeunt attendants*

DON PEDRO Come let us hence, and put on other weeds,   **30**
And then to Leonato's we will go.

CLAUDIO   And Hymen now with luckier issue speed's
Than this for whom we rendered up this woe.

[*Exeunt*

5:4

Benedick asks Leonato's permission to marry Beatrice. Claudio confirms his willingness to marry Hero's 'cousin' and discovers that she is Hero herself. Beatrice and Benedick realise they were tricked into love but nevertheless agree to marry.

3	*debated* discussed
5	*against her will* unintentionally
7	*sort* turn out
8	*by faith enforced* compelled by my pledge (to Beatrice)
9	*to a reckoning* to pay (i.e. with the duel)
14	*office* role
15	*be* pretend to be
17	*confirmed countenance* a straight face
18	*entreat your pains* beg to trouble you
20	*To bind me, or undo me* i.e. by marrying him to Beatrice (the metaphor recalls the idea of tying the marriage knot) *undo* ruin
23	*lent her* i.e. by means of the trick played on Beatrice in Act 3 Scene 1
24	*requite her* love her in return
25	*The sight whereof* i.e. the trick played on Benedick in Act 2 Scene 3
27	*enigmatical* difficult to understand
28	*your good will* your approval (for their marriage)
29	*May stand with ours* should agree with our desire to marry

*Don Pedro rebukes Benedick for his **February face** (line 41). Can you explain Benedick's mood – and how he reacts to Claudio and Don Pedro?*

- *Is he preoccupied with other thoughts: his own marriage; Leonato's words at lines 23 and 25–6?*
- *Does he still resent Claudio and Don Pedro's behaviour in disgracing Hero?*
- *What is Claudio and Don Pedro's tone: flippant, mocking, resentful, tactless, good-humoured? Do you find their tone surprising or inappropriate?*

36	*attend* wait for
	yet determined still resolved

5:4   *Enter* **Leonato, Antonio, Benedick, Beatrice, Hero,**
Margaret, Ursula, *and the* **Friar**

Friar   Did I not tell you she was innocent?

Leonato   So are the Prince and Claudio, who accused her
Upon the error that you heard debated.
But Margaret was in some fault for this,
Although against her will, as it appears   5
In the true course of all the question.

Antonio   Well, I am glad that all things sort so well.

Benedick   And so am I, being else by faith enforced
To call young Claudio to a reckoning for it.

Leonato   Well, daughter, and you gentlewomen all,   10
Withdraw into a chamber by yourselves,
And when I send for you come hither masked.
The Prince and Claudio promised by this hour
To visit me. You know your office, brother;
You must be father to your brother's daughter   15
And give her to young Claudio.

                                                    [*Exeunt all the women*

Antonio   Which I will do with confirmed countenance.

Benedick   Friar, I must entreat your pains, I think.

Friar   To do what, signor?

Benedick   To bind me, or undo me; one of them.   20
Signor Leonato, truth it is, good signor,
Your niece regards me with an eye of favour.

Leonato   That eye my daughter lent her; 'tis most true.

Benedick   And I do with an eye of love requite her.

Leonato   The sight whereof I think you had from me,   25
From Claudio and the Prince; but what's your will?

Benedick   Your answer, sir, is enigmatical.
But, for my will, my will is your good will
May stand with ours, this day to be conjoined
In the state of honourable marriage –   30
In which, good Friar, I shall desire your help.

Leonato   My heart is with your liking.

Friar   And my help.
Here comes the Prince and Claudio.

              Enter **Don Pedro** *and* **Claudio** *with attendant lords*

Don Pedro Good morrow to this fair assembly.

Leonato   Good morrow, Prince, good morrow, Claudio;   35
We here attend you. Are you yet determined

133

38 *I'll hold my mind* I won't change my mind
Ethiope black (fair skin was regarded as a mark of beauty)

41 *February face* i.e. sombre, serious

43 *the savage bull* Claudio reminds Benedick of the days when he scorned to be made a cuckold through marriage by quoting Benedick's own words against him (see Act 1 Scene 1 line 191).

46 *Europa* Europa's beauty prompted Jove to transform himself into a bull and carry her off to Crete on his back.

48 *an amiable low* an agreeable voice

49 *leaped your father's cow* i.e. mounted your mother

50 *noble feat* magnificent exploit (ironic)

52 *I owe you* I'll pay you back
reckonings debts (of honour)

63 *defiled* slandered

66 *but whiles* only as long as

67 *qualify* explain

69 *largely* in full

70 *let wonder seem familiar* become accustomed to amazement

71 *let us presently* let us go immediately

How should the unmasking episode be staged: with great solemnity, with some humour at Claudio's expense; as a serious test of his repentance? Might we suspect that Leonato could double-cross Claudio?

- *Might Hero be hideously disguised? Could she pretend to be awkward and unattractive? How?*
- *Would Beatrice, Margaret and Ursula also be masked – could there be some confusion?*
- *How does Claudio address the masked Hero: sincerely, resentfully, gently, coldly?*

72 *Soft and fair* wait a minute

	Today to marry with my brother's daughter?	
CLAUDIO	I'll hold my mind, were she an Ethiope.	
LEONATO	Call her forth, brother, here's the Friar ready.	

[*Exit* ANTONIO

DON PEDRO	Good morrow, Benedick; why, what's the matter,	40
	That you have such a February face	
	So full of frost, of storm and cloudiness?	
CLAUDIO	I think he thinks upon the savage bull.	
	Tush, fear not, man, we'll tip thy horns with gold,	
	And all Europa shall rejoice at thee,	45
	As once Europa did a lusty Jove	
	When he would play the noble beast in love.	
BENEDICK	Bull Jove, sir, had an amiable low,	
	And some such strange bull leaped your father's cow,	
	And got a calf in that same noble feat	50
	Much like to you, for you have just his bleat.	

Enter ANTONIO, *with the women masked*

CLAUDIO	For this I owe you. Here comes other reckonings.	
	Which is the lady I must seize upon?	
ANTONIO	This same is she, and I do give you her.	
CLAUDIO	Why then, she's mine. Sweet, let me see your face.	55
LEONATO	No, that you shall not till you take her hand	
	Before this Friar, and swear to marry her.	
CLAUDIO	Give me your hand before this holy Friar;	
	I am your husband, if you like of me.	
HERO [*Unmasking*]	And when I lived, I was your other wife;	60
	And when you loved, you were my other husband.	
CLAUDIO	Another Hero?	
HERO	Nothing certainer.	
	One Hero died defiled, but I do live,	
	And surely as I live, I am a maid.	
DON PEDRO	The former Hero, Hero that is dead?	65
LEONATO	She died, my lord, but whiles her slander lived.	
FRIAR	All this amazement can I qualify	
	When after that the holy rites are ended,	
	I'll tell you largely of fair Hero's death.	
	Meantime, let wonder seem familiar	70
	And to the chapel let us presently.	
BENEDICK	Soft and fair, Friar; which is Beatrice?	
BEATRICE [*Unmasking*]	I answer to that name. What is your will?	
BENEDICK	Do not you love me?	

74   *than reason*   than is reasonable

83   *friendly recompense*   as a friend

87   *halting*   limping, lame (i.e. the rhythm is uneven)

88   *Fashioned to*   shaped, created for

91   *our own hands against our hearts*   our own words contradicting our professed feelings

93–4   *upon great persuasion*   under great pressure

94–5   *in a consumption*   wasting away, pining (for love)

I will stop your mouth (line 96). Beatrice had used a similar expression in Act 2 Scene 1 (line 232). Compare the circumstances of the two occasions, particularly the part played by substitution, trickery and deception.

---

98   *a college of wit-crackers*   a whole school of comedians
flout   mock

99   *humour*   new disposition
care for a satire or an epigram   worry about a mocking poem or witticism

100   *beaten with brains*   defeated by mockery

100–1   *wear nothing handsome about him*   (i.e. won't attract attention to himself)

101–2   *think nothing to any purpose*   take no notice

102–3   *flout at me*   mock me

103   *giddy thing*   a changeable creature

105   *like to be*   about to become

107   *I had well hoped*   I was hoping

108   *cudgelled*   beaten
a double dealer   a married man (as opposed to a single man); an unfaithful husband; a hypocrite (having spoken against marriage for so long)

109–10   *do not look exceedingly narrowly to thee*   does not keep a very watchful eye on you

112   *lighten … our wives' heels*   a bawdy reference to the anticipated activities of the marriage bed

BEATRICE	Why no, no more than reason.

BENEDICK   Why, then your uncle, and the Prince, and Claudio   **75**
        Have been deceived; they swore you did.

BEATRICE   Do not you love me?

BENEDICK   Troth no, no more than reason.

BEATRICE   Why, then my cousin, Margaret and Ursula
        Are much deceived; for they did swear you did.

BENEDICK   They swore that you were almost sick for me.   **80**

BEATRICE   They swore that you were well-nigh dead for me.

BENEDICK   'Tis no such matter. Then you do not love me?

BEATRICE   No truly, but in friendly recompense.

LEONATO   Come, cousin, I am sure you love the gentleman.

CLAUDIO   And I'll be sworn upon't, that he loves her,   **85**
        For here's a paper written in his hand,
        A halting sonnet of his own pure brain
        Fashioned to Beatrice.

HERO   And here's another
        Writ in my cousin's hand, stol'n from her pocket,
        Containing her affection unto Benedick.   **90**

BENEDICK   A miracle! Here's our own hands against our hearts. Come, I will
        have thee; but, by this light, I take thee for pity.

BEATRICE   I would not deny you; but, by this good day, I yield upon great
        persuasion. And partly to save your life, for I was told you were in a
        consumption.   **95**

BENEDICK   Peace – I will stop your mouth. [*He kisses her*]

DON PEDRO   How dost thou, 'Benedick the married man'?

BENEDICK   I'll tell thee what, Prince: a college of witcrackers cannot flout me
        out of my humour. Dost thou think I care for a satire or an epigram?
        No. If a man will be beaten with brains, 'a shall wear nothing handsome   **100**
        about him. In brief, since I do purpose to marry, I will think nothing to
        any purpose that the world can say against it; and therefore never flout
        at me for what I have said against it; for man is a giddy thing, and this is
        my conclusion. For thy part, Claudio, I did think to have beaten thee;
        but in that thou art like to be my kinsman, live unbruised and love my   **105**
        cousin.

CLAUDIO   I had well hoped thou wouldst have denied Beatrice, that I might
        have cudgelled thee out of thy single life to make thee a double dealer;
        which out of question thou wilt be, if my cousin do not look exceeding
        narrowly to thee.   **110**

BENEDICK   Come, come, we are friends. Let's have a dance ere we are married,
        that we may lighten our own hearts and our wives' heels.

LEONATO   We'll have dancing afterward.

114 *music* musicians

116 *staff* staff of office symbolising authority (possibly, also, an elderly person's walking stick)
reverend respected
tipped with horn another reference to the cuckold's horns

117 *ta'en in flight* captured whilst trying to escape

118 *with* by

119 *brave* fine, excellent

Leonato agrees to Benedick's marrying Beatrice and directs the pre-nuptial ceremony. Claudio submits to Leonato's choice and discovers that Hero is alive. Benedick and Beatrice publicly acknowledge their love. News of Don John's capture only briefly mars the celebrations.

BENEDICK   First, of my word; therefore play, music.
Prince, thou art sad; get thee a wife, get thee a wife.   **115**
There is no staff more reverend than one tipped with horn.

Enter a **MESSENGER**

MESSENGER   My lord, your brother John is ta'en in flight
And brought with armed men back to Messina.

BENEDICK   Think not on him till tomorrow; I'll devise thee brave punishments
for him. Strike up, pipers.   **120**

Dance

[*Exeunt*

Much Ado About Nothing

List of other titles in this series:

2003 titles:

Henry IV Part One
Lawrence Green
0-7487-6960-9

Henry IV Part One Teacher Resource Book
Lawrence Green
0-7487-6968-4

Julius Caesar
Mark Morris
0-7487-6959-5

Julius Caesar Teacher Resource Book
Mark Morris
0-7487-6967-6

Macbeth
Dinah Jurksaitis
0-7487-6955-2

Macbeth Teacher Resource Book
Dinah Jurksaitis
0-7487-6961-7

The Merchant of Venice
Tony Farrell
0-7487-6957-9

The Merchant of Venice Teacher Resource book
Tony Farrell
0-7487-6963-3

Romeo and Juliet
Duncan Beal
0-7487-6956-0

Romeo and Juliet Teacher Resource Book
Duncan Beal
0-7487-6962-5

The Tempest
David Stone
0-7487-6958-7

The Tempest Teacher Resource Book
David Stone
0-7487-6965-X

2004 titles:

Antony and Cleopatra
Tony Farrell
0-7487-8602-3

Antony and Cleopatra Teacher Resource Book
Tony Farrell
0-7487-8606-6

A Midsummer Night's Dream
Dinah Jurksaitis
0-7487-8604-X

A Midsummer Night's Dream Teacher Resource Book
Dinah Jurksaitis
0-7487-8608-2

Much Ado About Nothing
Lawrence Green
0-7487-8607-4

Much Ado About Nothing Teacher Resource Book
Lawrence Green
0-7487-8603-1

Othello
Steven Croft
0-7487-8601-5

Othello Teacher Resource Book
Steven Croft
0-7487-8605-8